G000253868

Sean Moran, head chef and owner of landmark North Bondi restaurant Sean's Panaroma, has worked with some of Australia's most talented chefs, including Gay Bilson, Anders Ousback, Neil Perry and Stefano Manfredi.

According to *Sydney Morning Herald* restaurant reviewer Matthew Evans, Sean is 'the man you'd entrust to cook your last meal, balancing home-style comfort with modern tastes; his flavours make me go weak at the knees'.

let it simmer
Sean Moran

with photography by Simon Griffiths

LANTERN
an imprint of
PENGUIN BOOKS

LANTERN

Published by the Penguin Group
Penguin Group (Australia)
250 Camberwell Road, Camberwell, Victoria 3124, Australia
(a division of Pearson Australia Group Pty Ltd)
Penguin Group (USA) Inc.
375 Hudson Street, New York, New York 10014, USA
Penguin Group (Canada)
90 Eglinton Avenue East, Suite 700, Toronto ON M4P 2Y3, Canada
(a division of Pearson Penguin Canada Inc.)
Penguin Books Ltd
80 Strand, London WC2R 0RL, England
Penguin Ireland
25 St Stephen's Green, Dublin 2, Ireland
(a division of Penguin Books Ltd)
Penguin Books India Pvt Ltd
11 Community Centre, Panchsheel Park, New Delhi – 110 017, India
Penguin Group (NZ)
Cnr Airborne and Rosedale Roads, Albany, Auckland, New Zealand
(a division of Pearson New Zealand Ltd)
Penguin Books (South Africa) (Pty) Ltd
24 Sturdee Avenue, Rosebank, Johannesburg 2196, South Africa

Penguin Books Ltd, Registered Offices: 80 Strand, London, WC2R 0RL, England

First published by Penguin Group (Australia),
a division of Pearson Australia Group Pty Ltd, 2006

10 9 8 7 6 5 4 3 2 1

Text copyright © Sean Moran 2006
Photographs copyright © Simon Griffiths 2006

The moral right of the author has been asserted

All rights reserved. Without limiting the rights under copyright reserved above,
no part of this publication may be reproduced, stored in or introduced into
a retrieval system, or transmitted, in any form or by any means (electronic,
mechanical, photocopying, recording or otherwise), without the prior written
permission of both the copyright owner and the above publisher of this book.

Design by Debra Billson © Penguin Group (Australia)
Fabric design on cover copyright © Les Toiles du Soleil 2005
Back-cover photograph by Simon Griffiths
Props styling by Carlu Seaver
Page 71: 'To Make a Pearl' by M.F.K. Fisher. From Consider the Oyster. Included in THE
ART OF EATING. Published by Wiley Publishing, Inc. Copyright © 1941, 1954, 2004 by
M.F.K. Fisher. Reprinted with permission of Lescher & Lescher, Ltd. All rights reserved.
Typeset in PMN Caecilia and Avenir by Post Pre-press Group, Brisbane, Queensland
Colour reproduction by Splitting Image, Clayton, Victoria
Printed and bound in China by 1010 Printing International Ltd

National Library of Australia
Cataloguing-in-Publication data:

Moran, Sean (Sean Anthony).
  Let it simmer.

  Bibliography.
  Includes index.
  ISBN 1 920989 31 5.

  1. Cookery. I. Griffiths, Simon (Simon John). II. Title.

641.5

www.penguin.com.au

Dedicated to the memory of my mother,

Gail Ellen Provd, Moran, Hill, Mansell

Contents

lunch
Saturday + Sunday
12-3
dinner
Wednesday - Saturday
6.30 - 9.30

Introduction

*The most remarkable thing about my mother is that for 30 years
she served nothing but leftovers. The original meal was never found.*

Tracey Ullman

I lay no claim to an upbringing nurtured by gastronomic
delights: my mother was proud and headstrong, but she
had it tough. While our cupboards were usually bleak and
often met with tuts of disapproval, we really hit rock bottom
the night she served us Vegemite broth. Hers was conveyor-
belt cuisine, and featured brand names such as Carnation,
Gravox and Tang. Bubble 'n' squeak was the family favourite,
and it was occasionally followed by a colourful Aeroplane jelly
or some concoction from Sara Lee that Mum loved to top with
a dollop of Dessert Whip, which, she insisted, never went out
of date! Nonetheless, it always felt mutually comforting joining
Mum in her domesticity, even if it was just to get the lumps
out of the gravy.

Until the age of twelve, I ate food divorced from its origins.
A brutal primary-school trip to an abattoir opened my eyes
to the reality of how what we ate in suburban oblivion arrived
on our plates. I remember watching surgical men in gumboots,
in awe of the precision of their every cut and their masculine
lack of emotion as throats were slashed and innards pulled
before each animal was systematically slung onto a conveyor
belt of hooks passing overhead. Blood and guts aside, I look
to that poignant excursion as my first essential link with the
food chain.

At boarding school, 'gifts' in the refectory were divided
between eight from coveted aluminium trays. As ravenous
adolescents we devoured everything indiscriminately:
shepherd's pie with powdered mashed potato, meat 'frisbees',
and the weekly grey mutton roast with, yes, Gravox. There
was no joy behind the servery. It reeked of routine, although
I remember a monthly spark of creativity with the likes of
tinned peaches set in jelly.

I now thank these daily deprivations for fuelling my
private passion to cook. Somehow, albeit perversely, they
drew me in . . .

My professional cooking life began at the age of sixteen in
a gingham-clad 'provincial' restaurant in Surry Hills renowned
for serving snails and frogs' legs. Strangely, even the minced
garlic was imported from France! At the time, Sydney's most-
lauded restaurants were all inspired by French technique
and/or the nouvelle cuisine. I went on to spend my formative
years in such kitchens (where they all peeled and minced their
own garlic), besotted by the most dynamic of mentors – Martin
Teplitzky of Bon Cafard in Darlinghurst, and Gay Bilson and
Janni Kyritsis of Berowra Waters Inn.

A couple of my closest friends in the industry began
hatching an irresistible plan to open a modest restaurant
somewhere in the hills of Chianti, and despite the fact I'd never

been, I'd seen the pictures, and that was enough! We set off, filled with hope and romance, to live on the tightest of budgets yet managing to eat like kings. I'll never forget a head of buffalo mozzarella stuffed with ricotta and studded with white truffles from our local deli. The sheer beauty and ambrosial flavour of that slice of edible white 'terrazzo' nailed me to the cross – I'd simply never eaten handmade, agrarian food.

With the months slipping by and the heady flavours of each season sweeping us away, I found myself hopping back and forth between my two favourite countries, now totally obsessed with anything Italian. Back home in Sydney, I was temporarily adopted by Franca and Stefano Manfredi and their northern Italian restaurant in Ultimo, where I tapped into a wealth of deeply rooted kitchen traditions while I patiently waited and waited for news that the Chianti dream had been realised . . .

In the heady late 1980s the erudite Anders Ousback offered me the reins of his kitchen at Taylor Square Restaurant, and I was thrilled by the challenge of running my first 'brigade'. These were excessive times but, ironically, we were serving boarding-school-style 'comfort food', saluting the institution with the likes of eggs mayonnaise, corned beef with glazed carrot and mashed potato, and roast chook with bread sauce. Hundreds queued nightly down the stairs, sharing this yearning for lashings of honest, unadulterated food. This was extremely reassuring and the dishes I continue to serve remain a legacy to the confidence Anders breathed into my cooking.

In December 1993 Michael, my life partner, and I opened Sean's Panaroma, our 'salty jewel' of a restaurant at Bondi Beach. After a couple of awkwardly located (but fun) ventures in seedy pubs, we were drained financially, so the set up was a very beg-borrow-and-do-it-yourself affair. Invaluable friends joined a sheltered workshop, helping us to scrape away old paint, glue tiles, jackhammer, screw tables together, and scour auctions for second-hand chairs. Once the last letter of our sign was carved, painted and wired to the roof, the gas was lit.

For the first couple of years the cooking at Sean's was juggled between a three-bar, gas chargrill and my old enamelled Sydney Kooka, on top of which perched a small convection oven. Crockery and cutlery were salvaged from our first dining-room, along with a second-hand ice-cream machine (which still works today, touch wood). Without the luxury of a cool room, we relied entirely on bench refrigeration, which simply meant that we bought more regularly and that any spare surface boasted an abundance of ripening produce – a handsome alternative to floral displays. All washing up was done by hand in a second-hand four-sink stand. The reality was that we could only budget for a grease arrestor, exhaust system and a few pots 'n' pans!

I remember our charmingly modest stack of worm farms in the alleyway, and the dainty buckets for compost that some folk turned their noses up at. The council bloke literally went cross-eyed when we asked if we could use the grey water from the hand sink to flush the dunny! So, it's an understatement to say some thought us far too rebellious: we were unlicensed, refused credit cards, and wouldn't let anyone smoke. Customers had to come up to the kitchen to give their order, and on Thursday, Friday and Saturday nights we gave them no choice at all. Eyebrows were constantly raised at the bleak look of the place (one food critic described it as 'like being in a bomb shelter in Bosnia') but we were doin' it for ourselves and we were really cookin'!

From the beginning, main courses in the restaurant have been served as one would serve them at home: protein with carbohydrates and vegetables – comforting, complete meals. Our menu is chalked on individual blackboards that hang above the kitchen and, apart from a few 'signature' dishes, may change seasonally, weekly or even mid-service. The style of our cooking is widely categorised as being 'modern Australian', although I feel 'Anglo-Italian' is perhaps more accurate, given

my Mediterranean obsession. Having said that, I pride myself on our humble little 'bunker' being so warmly embraced as a congenial arena for Australia's freshest seasonal produce.

Each week for the past ten years Michael and I have been lugging kitchen scraps from the restaurant up to our shack in the Blue Mountains to help feed our dozen chooks and top up the compost pile for our modest 'cook's' garden. Most of our block is native bush, the top two hectares blessed with basalt soil. Our two dozen fruit trees are now at exciting stages of maturity after endless seasons of constant nurturing with organic feeds and mulch (a mate nicknamed me 'Nurtch' for this apparent neurosis – 'When you're not feeding people you're feeding bloody plants!' he'll bark).

Yields are mutually rewarding. Sometimes we return to the coast with a bundle of herbs for the restaurant, and there are usually various vegetables or a few eggs for friends. We have faith in this karmic cycle, knowing that one day scraps will morph their way back to the restaurant table as, perhaps, asparagus spears! I cherish this close relationship between the garden and the plate, and feel deeply privileged to be part of it all.

With the door ajar on restaurant kitchens, sharing recipes with loyal customers and food enthusiasts has to take on a personal perspective. For me, it is only in my professional world of restaurant cooking that accurate, step-by-step documenting and consistency become essential. However, when you meet the meals I cook in our shack in the mountains – as stories interwoven through this book – perhaps you will notice that there are no real recipes, no exacting quantities or time frames. My aim is to share an active process of cooking that relies entirely on senses and instinct.

The recipes and stories in the book are the result of osmosis, as no dish can ever claim to be entirely 'new'. Many reflect my hankering for honest, home-style cooking, while others started life in a backyard, shack or fishing boat, yet have snuggled their way into our restaurant. Naturally, they alter slightly each time they're prepared, by virtue of season, whim and the character of one's very own hand. With this in mind, I urge the reader to look at any recipe as a guideline. Absorb my kitchen propositions, let them 'simmer', then your own cooking will sparkle and seduce with the subtleties of personal interpretation. I hope this book brings out a little bit of the professional chef in the home cook – and vice versa.

Finally, if I may share one mantra that affects what I produce and ultimately how I nourish myself: sweep through your door free of any ill thoughts, for a happy cook cooks best!

Sean Moran

PS Oh, my friends eventually managed to open their little restaurant in the hills of Chianti. It offered a valuable cultural exchange 'program' not only for me but for colleagues here in Sydney for many years – an oasis in the increasingly fickle world of food, and a reminder that simplicity wins every time.

Almond Granola

For the most wholesome start to a day I choose organic,
preferably GM-free, oats toasted with almonds, olive oil and
honey. This granola keeps its crunch for weeks if you slip
a square of absorbent paper under the lid of your jar.

SERVES **15**

750 g organic rolled oats
250 ml honey
250 ml olive oil
100 g almonds (preferably with skins on)

1   Preheat oven to 150°C. Toss oats in a large sieve to remove
any fine dust. Melt honey with olive oil over a gentle flame in
a large non-stick baking tray. Add oats and almonds, stirring
to coat evenly, then bake for 15 minutes.

2   Stir, then return to oven and reset timer for another
15 minutes – repeat this process until granola is evenly toasted
and deep golden, about 1 hour. Remove tray and leave granola
to cool, uncovered, before storing in an airtight jar.

For an extra textural explosion,
try scattering a bowl of granola
with a handful of blueberries,
then top with a dollop of sheep's
milk yoghurt. ⟶

Malt Scrolls

The idea for these addictive scrolls came via a recipe in Carol Field's book *The Italian Baker*. A bread from Como in northern Italy, it is traditionally proved in baskets and sold as a loaf 'excellent for breakfast'. At the restaurant we form the dough into double scrolls and adore the sweet malty flavour any time of the day.

Using a starter made with milk and barley malt gives these scrolls a rich caramel bloom. Once formed, the scrolls are chilled overnight, wrapped in plastic to prevent the dough from drying out. This slow maturation produces a fine, blistering crust when baked. Make sure you read through the recipe before you start so that you understand the timing.

MAKES 6 DOUBLE SCROLLS

625 g unbleached baker's flour
1 scant tablespoon salt
250 ml tepid water

STARTER
1 heaped teaspoon dried yeast
1 heaped tablespoon barley malt
50 ml tepid water
100 ml milk
100 g unbleached baker's flour

1   To make the starter, whisk yeast, malt and tepid water together in a small bowl. Meanwhile, warm milk to blood temperature, then add yeast mixture and beat in flour for about 100 strokes until smooth. Transfer starter to a 1–2 litre plastic bucket with a tight-fitting lid and leave to ferment unrefrigerated for at least 4 hours but preferably overnight.

2   To make the dough, sift flour and salt onto your bench, then form a well in the centre. Pour in starter and water and bring mixture together with your hands to make a dough. Knead for 10–15 minutes until smooth – think baby's bum! Transfer dough to a large, lightly oiled bowl, then cover with plastic film and allow to prove in a warm spot until doubled in size – this will take about 1½ hours.

3   Return dough to lightly floured bench and knead for 5–10 minutes. Using a rolling pin, roll out dough, dusting it with just enough flour to stop it sticking, until about 20 cm long and 1 cm thick. Using a large knife, cut dough lengthways into 6 long strips. Take one strip of dough and roll the top half on a slight angle to produce an exaggerated, spiralling scroll. Roll the bottom part of the strip to produce another roll – you should end up with an S-shaped double scroll. Arrange scrolls on 2 baking trays lined with baking paper, then dust with flour. Insert the trays into plastic bags, loosely tucking any excess under trays, then refrigerate overnight.

4   Next day, remove scrolls from fridge and put somewhere cosy away from draughts (the perfect place in my kitchen is on the wire rack suspended over my stove with a gently simmering pot below!). Leave to prove for 45 minutes–1 hour until doubled in size.

5   Meanwhile, preheat oven to 250°C. Remove trays from their bags. Spray scrolls with a fine mist of warm water, then dust tops with flour and put quickly into oven. Close door, reduce temperature to 200°C and bake for 35–45 minutes until scrolls are deep golden brown. Slide onto a wire rack to cool, then pull scrolls apart to serve.

Cracked-wheat Logs

This comforting, earthy bread owes much of its success to a little gem of a book titled *Better than Store Bought*, and to the friend that brought it into our very first kitchen. The coarse cracked wheat or burghul, cooked by absorption before being added to the dough, adds moisture and a wonderful even texture. Apart from the shaping of the loaves, my only other tweaking of the recipe has been the sesame crust – a personal preference to rolling the dough in whole grains of wheat. I'm sure you too will be hooked by this wholesome loaf from the very first slice.

MAKES 2 LOGS

100 g cracked wheat (burghul)
½ teaspoon salt
2 teaspoons soft brown sugar
2 teaspoons dried yeast
50 ml tepid water
½ cup sesame seeds

DOUGH
750 g unbleached baker's flour
190 g wholemeal plain flour
½ cup unprocessed bran
1½ tablespoons salt
50 ml olive oil
400 ml tepid water

1   Bring 250 ml water to a boil over a moderate flame in a small, heavy-based saucepan, then stir in cracked wheat and salt. Cover and lower heat, then simmer gently for about 15–20 minutes until all water has been absorbed and wheat is tender (you may need a simmer mat). Pour onto a tray and leave to cool to room temperature.

2   Meanwhile, whisk brown sugar, yeast and 50 ml tepid water together in a small bowl, then set aside for about 10 minutes until foaming.

3   To make the dough, sift baker's flour into a bowl, then stir in wholemeal flour and bran. Tip the lot onto your bench and make a well in the centre. Transfer softened cracked wheat to bowl, then stir in yeast mixture, salt, oil and 400 ml tepid water until combined. Tip cracked-wheat mixture into well in flour and bring together to form a firm dough, then knead for 10–15 minutes until smooth. Put dough into a large, lightly oiled bowl, then cover with plastic film and leave in a cosy, draught-free spot to prove until doubled in size, about 1–1½ hours.

4   Tip dough out onto bench and knead for 5–10 minutes, then divide into 2 even pieces. Roll each piece of dough into a smooth log about the length of a rolling pin. Scatter sesame seeds over a tray, then roll logs in seeds until well coated and seeds are embedded. Transfer logs to a baking tray lined with baking paper, or to troughs if you have them, then cover with plastic film and leave for a final, cosy prove for about 1 hour until doubled in size.

5   Meanwhile, preheat oven to 250°C. Spray logs with a fine mist of warm water and put quickly into oven. Close door, reduce temperature to 200°C and bake for 45–50 minutes until deep golden brown. Slide onto a wire rack to cool.

Walnut and Raisin Bread

This highly aromatic fruit and nut bread is baked on a slightly lower heat than other breads due to the honey in the dough. You can make, bake and eat all on the same day, although I reckon this makes even better toasting bread, spread with a soft cheese such as fresh ricotta.

MAKES 1 LOAF

150 g freshly shelled walnuts

1 teaspoon dried yeast

160 ml tepid water

2 tablespoons honey

2 tablespoons walnut oil

½ teaspoon salt

300 g unbleached baker's flour

100 g raisins

1 egg yolk

1 tablespoon pouring cream

1 Preheat oven to 180°C. Roast walnuts on a baking tray for 7–8 minutes until golden brown. Tip nuts onto a clean tea towel, then bring up sides and rub nuts vigorously with cloth to loosen skins. Pick out nuts (they will have crumbled slightly) and leave to cool. Discard skins.

2 Whisk yeast, warm water, honey, walnut oil, salt and just enough flour to make a smooth batter, then leave in a warm place to swell for 15–20 minutes. Tip remaining flour into a food processor with a quarter of the walnuts and whiz to a coarse meal. Tip mixture onto a clean workbench, forming a well in centre. Pour in yeast mixture and bring together with floured hands. Knead for several minutes before incorporating remaining walnuts and raisins, then knead for a further 7–10 minutes until elastic.

3 Lightly rub a bowl at least double the size of the dough with a drizzle of walnut oil. Roll dough around to grease up its surface, then cover bowl with plastic film or a damp towel and leave to prove in a warm place for 1–1½ hours until doubled in size.

4 Knead dough for 5 minutes, then form into a smooth, round loaf and put on a baking tray lined with baking paper. Leave to prove again in a warm place for about 45 minutes, covered as previously, until doubled in size.

5 Meanwhile, preheat oven to 180°C. Make a glaze by lightly mixing egg yolk with cream, then paint evenly over bread with a pastry brush. Swiftly slide loaf into oven and cook for 30–40 minutes until a deep caramel. Allow to cool to room temperature on a wire rack before slicing.

Lentil Patties

These wholesome lentil patties are irresistible eaten hot straight from the pan, but are also great cold on a picnic with chutney and a few salad leaves.

SERVES **4–6**

200 g brown lentils (preferably organic Australian)

1 large onion

4 cloves garlic

250 ml olive oil

1 bay leaf

salt

1 handful flat-leaf parsley

1 handful mint

zest and juice of 1 lemon

1 tablespoon cumin seeds

50 g finely grated parmesan (preferably grana padano)

250 g cottage cheese

1 handful coarse fresh breadcrumbs

freshly ground black pepper

plain flour, for dusting

1 egg

100 ml milk

2 handfuls fine fresh
   breadcrumbs

1 Soak lentils in cold water for 2 hours, then drain and check thoroughly for any tiny stones. Peel and finely dice onion and garlic. Heat 50 ml of the olive oil in a small saucepan, then add onion and garlic and sauté for several minutes until pale golden. Pour in 100 ml cold water, then add lentils, bay leaf and 1 teaspoon salt and bring to a boil. Reduce to a simmer and cook for 20–30 minutes until lentils are tender and all water has been absorbed. Pour lentils into a large bowl, removing bay leaf, and leave to cool to room temperature.

2 Meanwhile, wash, pick and coarsely chop parsley and mint leaves, then add to lentils with lemon zest and juice. In a small dry frying pan, toast cumin seeds over a low flame until fragrant, then cool and grind. Mix ground cumin through lentils with parmesan, cottage cheese and coarse breadcrumbs, then season to taste with salt and pepper. Form mixture into small patties 5–6 cm in diameter and 1 cm thick, then refrigerate for 1–2 hours before crumbing.

3 Lightly dust patties with flour. Lightly whisk egg with milk. Dip patties in eggwash, then drain well and dip in fine breadcrumbs on both sides and around edges. Heat remaining olive oil in a large frying pan over a moderate flame, then carefully lower in patties and shallow-fry until deep golden on both sides. Drain on paper towel before serving hot, or leave to cool for a picnic. In both cases, serve the patties with Red Pepper Chutney (see page 202) and a salad.

Brown Rice and Vegetable Pie

During a grave illness many years ago, a friend gave me *Zen Macrobiotic Cooking*, an enlightening book by Japanese Buddhist monk Michel Abehsera. These pages spoke logically about the seesaw of nourishment and how everything we eat is either acid (yin – sugar) or alkaline (yang – salt). Of all the foods we eat, brown rice is the only one that boasts the perfect balance of the two, so I began a mission to try to enjoy eating the stuff. With this philosophy in mind, a little cook's curiosity and an addictive sesame salt known as 'gomasio', I embellished the brown rice idea, building layer upon layer until satiated by this wholesome pie. From the creamed sweet potato blanket down to the crisp sesame base, each layer plays a supporting textural (and nutritional) role. I hope you find it well worth the effort, and a joy to digest.

1 quantity Savoury Shortcrust Pastry (see page 199)

2 tablespoons sunflower seeds

1 teaspoon cumin seeds

300 g brown rice

1 teaspoon Gomasio (see page 196)

1 kg sweet potatoes

125 g butter

salt

2 red onions

4 cloves garlic

500 g burstingly ripe tomatoes

750 ml olive oil

2 tablespoons balsamic vinegar

freshly ground black pepper

1 handful basil leaves

2 aubergines

1 tablespoon plain flour

500 g pine-forest mushrooms (slippery Jacks or saffron milkcaps) *or* large field mushrooms

6 generous handfuls spinach

¼ small Savoy cabbage

150 g finely grated parmesan (preferably grana padano)

1 Preheat oven to 200°C. Line a 35 cm wide × 5 cm deep pie dish (or a springform or flan tin, if you want to turn it out) with pastry and bake until deep golden, following the instructions on page 199.

2 In a dry frying pan over a moderate flame, toast sunflower seeds for several minutes until golden, stirring to avoid burning, then set aside. Toast cumin seeds similarly, then grind when cool.

3 Wash rice, then put it into a medium-sized, heavy-based saucepan and bring to a boil with 750 ml cold water. Reduce to a simmer, then cover and cook gently for 45 minutes until tender. Leave in pan to cool. Mix toasted sunflower seeds and gomasio through cooled rice.

4 While rice is cooking, peel sweet potatoes, then cut them into even rounds and bring to a boil in a saucepan of water. Reduce to a moderate simmer and cook until just tender, then drain well before puréeing with butter until smooth. Season to taste with salt and keep warm.

5 Peel onions and cut into 5 cm chunks. Peel and mince garlic, then divide into thirds and set aside. Blanch and peel tomatoes, then dice. Heat 75 ml olive oil in a deep frying pan and sauté onion over a moderate flame until caramelised. Add a third of the minced garlic, then deglaze pan with vinegar. Add tomato, then season and cook until reduced to a sauce consistency. Tear basil leaves over surface, then mix in. Tip into a bowl and keep warm. Wash and dry frying pan.

6 Peel aubergines and cut lengthways into 1 cm slices. Sprinkle with salt, then leave to sweat for about 10 minutes before drying with paper towel and lightly dusting with flour. Heat 500 ml olive oil in frying pan over moderate heat and fry aubergine in batches, turning carefully, until deep golden brown on both sides. Drain well on paper towel. Wash and dry frying pan.

7 Use a dry pastry brush to remove any pine needles and dirt from mushrooms, then cut into 3 mm slices. Heat 100 ml olive oil in frying pan, then add mushrooms and season with salt and pepper. Sauté until deep golden, then, at the last moment, add second batch of garlic and remove pan from heat. Tip mushrooms into a bowl and keep warm. Wash and dry frying pan.

8 Remove stalks from spinach leaves, then wash and dry. Cut away and discard core from cabbage, then cut cabbage into thick slices. Heat 75 ml olive oil in frying pan over a moderate flame, then add cabbage and ground cumin and sauté lightly for several moments, shaking pan often until lightly coloured yet still slightly crisp. Season. Add spinach leaves and remaining garlic and cook for a second or two to wilt, then swiftly remove pan from heat.

9 Preheat oven to 200°C. To construct the pie, gently press rice into pastry case. Layer mushrooms evenly over rice, then spoon in tomato sauce and sprinkle with half the parmesan. Cover with aubergine slices, taking them right out to edges, then add cabbage and spinach. Scatter over remaining parmesan. Spread top flamboyantly with sweet potato, using a spatula to create little 'licks' of purée, then bake for about 30 minutes until deep golden. Allow pie to cool to room temperature (although you can serve it warm too) before cutting into wedges and serving with a green salad.

The Dance Of The Paella

Even though the Lima beans are swollen from their overnight soak, and a pile of supplies is to hand, there's still much to organise before our real paella dance can begin.

We're expecting about twenty, so we're having to improvise. Out in our garden, circles of bricks are at the ready, stacked neatly to hug the girth of our pan. There are slight gaps for air, and a pile of twigs teetering through to logs is arranged inside.

Back in the kitchen I set handfuls of soaked beans on for a slow boil in a pan of fresh water. A bucket of tiny clams needs a good tumble under the running tap before I leave the shells to purge in more fresh water. Meanwhile, I peel, devein and then cut a couple of dozen prawns in half down their length. Next, I chop ten chicken thighs into large, bite-sized chunks, before stripping the skin off five chorizos, quartering them lengthways and cutting them to roughly the same size.

I peel and coarsely dice half-a-dozen onions, then push the same amount of tomatoes into the bean pan for a quick blanch before peeling and dicing them too. After I peel the whole head of garlic, I smash the cloves to a paste with the back of my knife and a little coarse salt for grip. A large vase of parsley is next for the chop, along with a fine grating of zest from three lemons.

I set up my tray with the dishes and tubs filled with my labouring. The beans remain stubborn as I head for the shelves to nab the little tin of sweet paprika and my tiny envelope of saffron threads. I tuck in the salt, pepper grinder and bottle of olive oil, then I'm off to the fridge for a bucket of chook stock.

The few handfuls of peas need podding, when I remember the kilo of rice, all plump, snug and clothed in its bag. Between dealing with the beans, peas and rice there's a rap at the door, and in no time our fire is lit!

I set my three-litre bucket of stock on the stove to boil, then get a bit theatrical with a branch of rosemary on my way out the back. Flames seduce our guests and, by the time they've mellowed, it's the size of the pan (not my bulging tray of preparations) that has everyone's attention. A gay swirl of oil gets things started, any minglers hit with the first waft of sizzling sausage and onion. My next lure is the huge wave of garlic, then the sound of raining rice. Lumps of chicken, doused in salt, pepper, paprika and saffron, get tossed around the pan with my branch, now a huge social magnet to all.

The fierce HISSSSS of the boiling stock calls for another layer of bricks to be added so things can snuggle in to simmer, then I lay my fragrant branch in the centre of the pan. We scatter in the peas and tomato, waltzing around the pan for 10 minutes or so, a prod and a shake here and there as we go . . .

As the rice sucks away at the juices it feels time to top up
with a drizzle more stock. Ravenous hands dig at the clams,
helping to spread and poke 'em all into the surface. Within
minutes the shells have burst open, our cue to scatter over
the prawns, parsley and lemon, tucking the beans into any
last pockets of syrup as we go.

In a few more minutes, our dance is almost done...
But having heaved our feast from the coals, we have a
torturous 10-minute wait while our crust releases its grip on
the base of the pan. Then, just as my troupe is growling to
mutiny, I insist (as choreographer) on several sharp twists
to set our crust free. All matters of decorum and grace are
abandoned and we tuck in, wildly scooping and licking and
sucking the shells.

*The whole garden, steeped in the pan's
sweet smoky aroma, erupts with greedy
shouts of 'The paella is cooked!'*

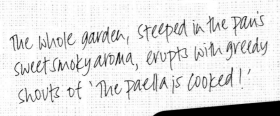

Linguine with Shredded Rocket, Lemon, Chilli and Parmesan

This 'signature' linguine has been a staple on the menu at Sean's Panaroma since we opened in 1993, after appearing previously in our 'dining-rooms' in the Grand and George hotels. It remains a tribute to my first taste of wild arugula, gathered from the hills of Fiesole in Italy in 1985. How excited I was to discover 'rocket' available commercially here in Sydney a year or so later. Who could now imagine life without this peppery salad green?

In cooler months I sometimes add a few chunks of slow-roasted pumpkin, although the original really needs no further embellishment. Feel free to play with various (ideally long) types of pasta.

SERVES 4

4 generous handfuls rocket
1 × 200 g piece parmesan (preferably grana padano)
1 lemon
2 cloves garlic
150 ml Chilli Oil (see page 195)
salt
400 g linguine
freshly ground black pepper

1   Three-quarters fill a large saucepan with cold water and bring to a boil. Meanwhile, wash, shake dry and then coarsely shred rocket. Coarsely grate parmesan. Squeeze and strain juice from lemon, then mince garlic and combine with lemon juice and chilli oil in a bowl large enough to toss linguine.

2   Throw a handful of cooking salt into the boiling water and let it return to a boil. Cook pasta for the time recommended on the packet until al dente, separating strands occasionally with a pair of tongs and testing towards end of time. Lift pasta into prepared bowl, draining it as you go yet taking a slight drizzle of the cooking water with the pasta (this will lubricate and combine dressing). Add shredded rocket and parmesan, then season and toss together before serving.

Orecchiette with Aged Pecorino, Pancetta and Peas

As a break from the traditional sauce of broccoli, cauliflower, chilli and anchovies served in Puglia, I like these 'little ears' loosely 'stuffed' with peas or chick peas, a dice of leg ham, pancetta or crumbled sausage.

SERVES **4–6**
1 × 150 g piece pancetta
4 cloves garlic
1 × 80 g piece well-aged pecorino
1 generous handful basil leaves
salt
150 g freshly shelled *or* frozen peas
1 tablespoon olive oil
200 ml pouring cream
freshly ground black pepper

DOUGH
160 g fine semolina
300 g unbleached baker's flour
½ teaspoon salt
170 ml tepid water

1　To make the dough, sift semolina, flour and salt onto your workbench and make a well in the centre. Pour in water and bring sides together with a fork until mixture is 'scraggy' (just coming together). Scrape up dough stuck to bench, then knead dough well for 5–8 minutes until smooth. Wrap in plastic film and refrigerate for at least 30 minutes.

2　Roll a small handful of the rested dough into a long log with a diameter of about 1 cm, then cut log into 2 mm thick discs. Dip thumb(s) in flour, then press each disc firmly, using a rolling motion to curl and so make a 'little ear'. As you make them, put orecchiette on a large board or tray dusted with semolina to dry for at least 1 hour – it is imperative to dry the pasta long enough so it retains its shape when boiled.

3　Bring a large saucepan of water to a boil. Meanwhile, cut pancetta into small dice. Peel and roughly chop garlic. Finely grate pecorino. Pound basil leaves in a mortar and pestle until almost a smooth paste.

4　Throw a handful of cooking salt into the boiling water and let it return to a boil before sliding in orecchiette. Set timer for 3 minutes, then add peas if fresh (at last minute if frozen) and let pot return to a boil, then cook for another 2–3 minutes until pasta is al dente and peas are tender.

5　While pasta is cooking, heat olive oil in a large frying pan over a moderate flame and sauté pancetta for several seconds until deeply caramelised, then add garlic and cook for several more seconds until golden. Deglaze pan with cream, then add basil and reduce slightly over heat to a light saucing consistency. Remove pan from heat. Check pasta is al dente, then drain and add to pan with a drizzle of cooking water. Toss together with pecorino and season to taste before serving.

A hint of pungency from an aged pecorino melted through the sauce adds a luxurious depth, and the charming little pasta cups are also fun to make.

Pici

The first time I tried these charming, irregular hand-rolled noodles was in a tiny osteria in the Tuscan hillside village of Montalcino. It was the texture of these jumping noodles that first grabbed me. Springy, pale and wormlike, they were rolled through coarsely chopped tomato that had been lightly stewed with a touch of dried chilli and some fruity extra-virgin olive oil and were scattered with a handful of finely grated pecorino. It remains the most memorable bowl of pasta I have ever had.

Well, I tried, of course, to make pici numerous times after this meal, endlessly frustrated by the way each strand would wrestle and spring back as I tried to roll it. Only recently I unearthed a recipe, thanks to Paul Bertolli and his inspiring book *Cooking by Hand*. It all makes sense now. The secret is not to work the gluten in the dough. No eggs are used (hence the paleness), and a little olive oil lends an added silkiness that helps with rolling.

The ripest tomatoes, stewed as I had them in Montalcino, are hard to beat with pici, but you could also try substituting these noodles for the linguine in the recipe on page 23. Another favourite is to pan-fry batons of aubergine in olive oil with garlic and stinging nettles before adding chopped ripe tomato. Then there is a roasted tomato sauce, or a hand-minced bolognaise, or . . . or . . .

I find it's best to cook these noodles fresh, as the texture changes somewhat as they dry.

SERVES **4–6**
350 g unbleached baker's flour
175 ml tepid water
25 ml extra-virgin olive oil
salt

1   Put the flour on a clean workbench, then drizzle it with water and extra-virgin olive oil, using a pastry scraper to help catch liquids and 'chop' them into the flour. Use your fingers to bring the dough together just enough to incorporate, then wrap in plastic film and refrigerate for about 1 hour.

2   Bring a large saucepan of water to a boil. Meanwhile, keeping the dough covered, tear off a small blob and roll gently on a flour-free area until about 40 cm long and 3–4 mm thick, pinching off each length and re-using excess dough until all dough has been used. Transfer pici to a lightly floured board as you make them.

3   Throw a handful of cooking salt into the boiling water and let it return to a boil before sliding in pici. Cook for 6 minutes until al dente, and serve with your chosen sauce.

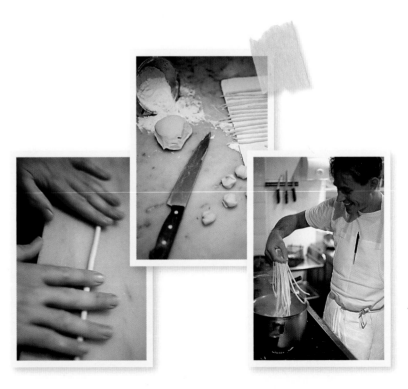

Saffron Pasta Coins with Sautéed Bugs and Tomato

Whether you get hold of the tapering-headed Moreton Bay, round-topped Balmain or similarly shaped deep-sea bugs, ensure they haven't been cooked. As the meat quickly turns a dull grey after death, bugs need to be cooked or frozen within several hours of being caught. Your most likely purchase, then, will be frozen green (uncooked) bugs, but sometimes one can be lucky enough to purchase live bugs, full of vigorous flap.

Originally from Genoa, these pasta 'coins' are traditionally stamped on both sides with wooden 'corzetti stampati'. Years back, while working in the Manfredi kitchen, I was lucky enough to be able to watch Franca Manfredi, the amazing matriarch of pasta makers, and her finely honed hands at work. This was something to behold! With a press from each finger and a flick of the wrist, her more personalised coins flew across a lightly dusted bench, all slightly irregular and utterly charming. I dedicate my version to her, and the way she inspired me.

SERVES **4–6**

8 green Moreton, Balmain or deep-sea bugs
1 large burstingly ripe tomato (preferably oxheart)
2 cloves garlic
1 bird's-eye chilli
1 generous handful basil
salt
200 g freshly shelled *or* frozen peas
150 ml extra-virgin olive oil
12 paper-thin slices flat pancetta
freshly ground black pepper
150 ml dry white wine
finely grated zest and juice of 1 lemon

SAFFRON COINS
300 g unbleached baker's flour
1 tablespoon salt
1 pinch saffron threads
3 eggs
salt
extra-virgin olive oil

1   To make the coins, sift flour onto a clean workbench with salt, then rub through saffron and form a well in the centre. Beat in eggs with a fork, gradually bringing in flour until all incorporated, then knead for several minutes to form a smooth dough. Wrap in plastic film and refrigerate for at least 30 minutes.

2   Roll dough into a log about 2 cm in diameter, then cut into 2 mm thick discs. Dip your forefinger and thumb in flour, then press each disc to form a deep indent on each side. As you make them, put coins on a large board or tray dusted with flour (note that you don't have to rest these before cooking, as you do the orecchiette). Bring a saucepan of well-salted water to a boil, then plunge in coins and cook for about 6 minutes until al dente, double-checking by biting one in half. Refresh under cool, running water, then drain and toss gently with a little extra-virgin olive oil to prevent sticking.

3   Lay each bug on its back and insert a small sharp knife into head where top part of shell meets tail. With a persuasive twist of your knife, free tail. Using sharp scissors, carefully snip down each side (avoid cutting tail meat). Hold middle firmly where small bowel duct sits at bottom of tail and carefully pull out body meat – the bowel trail will stay in the shell. Cut each bug into 6 bite-sized pieces.

4   Blanch and peel tomato, then cut into 5 mm dice. Peel and coarsely chop garlic. Finely chop chilli and pick basil leaves into tiny pieces.

5   Ten minutes before serving, bring a small saucepan of salted water to a boil, then throw in fresh peas for 5 minutes. Meanwhile, heat a large frying pan over a full flame with just enough of the extra-virgin olive oil to line the bottom. When hot, cook pancetta for several seconds on both sides until crisp, then drain on paper towel. Swiftly add bugmeat to pan, then season well and turn as each piece lightly colours – this will only take 30 seconds. Add saffron coins, garlic and chilli and sauté for several seconds until garlic is golden, then deglaze pan with wine, tomato and lemon juice. Sprinkle in lemon zest, basil, remaining olive oil and the drained peas, then swirl pan to combine sauce. Serve at once, scattered with coarsely crumbled pancetta.

Semolina Gnocchi, Roasted with Blue Cheese Sauce

The famous semolina-based gnocchi alla Romana bake to a beautiful crust and can be stored for a day or two with great success, wrapped in the slab in the fridge. Traditionally, these gnocchi are cut into rounds, which is great in a restaurant situation as a staff meal can be made of the 'unpresentable' offcuts. You may find a rectangle to be the best choice at home . . .

For a warming winter meal, I like to serve these puffed-up gnocchi baked crisp in a swathe of heady blue cheese sauce with a leafy salad on the side.

SERVES **8**

1 onion

1 clove garlic

2 cloves

1 handful parsley stalks

300 ml milk

300 ml pouring cream

150 g blue cheese (Milawa Blue, for example)

salt

freshly ground black pepper

SEMOLINA GNOCCHI

1 litre milk

1 bay leaf

freshly grated nutmeg

225 g coarse semolina

50 g finely grated parmesan (preferably grana padano)

25 g unsalted butter

4 egg yolks

finely grated zest of 1 lemon

salt

freshly ground white pepper

1 Line a 14 cm wide × 28 cm long and at least 15 mm deep baking tray with baking paper. To make gnocchi, bring milk, bay leaf and a few gratings of nutmeg to a boil in a saucepan over a moderate flame. Reduce to a simmer and gently 'rain' in semolina while beating with a wooden spoon. Cook, stirring, for 5–6 minutes until all the milk has been absorbed and the mixture pulls away from the sides of pot in one mass. Remove from heat, then discard bay leaf and beat in parmesan, butter, egg yolks, lemon zest, salt and pepper until well incorporated. Swiftly pour into lined tray and cover immediately with plastic film to avoid a crust forming, smoothing surface by pressing gently with hands, then leave to cool.

2 Meanwhile, make the sauce. Peel and thinly slice onion and peel and lightly crush garlic, then add to a saucepan with cloves, parsley stalks, milk and cream and bring to a boil over a moderate flame. Reduce to a simmer and cook gently for about 1 hour, then, using a wooden spoon, push firmly through a fine-meshed strainer over a bowl, discarding solids. Cut cheese into rough 1 cm cubes, then mix through hot sauce to melt. Season to taste.

3 Preheat oven to 180°C. Grease a shallow casserole or gratin dish with butter. Lift semolina slab out of tray and cut into 5 cm rounds (or rectangles) using a biscuit cutter or small glass (or knife) dipped in cold water, then arrange, slightly overlapping like roof tiles, in prepared dish. Pour cheese sauce over top and bake for 25 minutes until nicely crusted and golden, then serve.

Polenta with Braised Fennel and Olives

When making polenta I like to freshen up its flavour and texture by adding grated corn to the pot. Once crisped, the polenta makes a great mop for all the juices. Most polenta recipes call for constant stirring, but not this one. Keeping the lid on stops a crust forming on the surface, and the fine crust left on the bottom of the pot can be soaked off. Better still, scrape it off – if you're lucky enough it may come away in one wonderful piece (if it's been left to cool to room temperature) and makes a very tasty snack or edible serving bowl!

SERVES **4–6**

½ teaspoon fennel seeds

2 large bulbs fennel (with a few young, feathery tips)

125 ml extra-virgin olive oil

2 cloves garlic

125 ml tomato passata

125 ml dry white wine

125 ml Chook or Vegetable Stock (see pages 190–1)

finely grated zest and juice of ½ lemon

3 sprigs thyme

1 bay leaf

1 handful of your favourite olives (mine are Ligurian), pitted

salt

freshly ground black pepper

POLENTA

1 cob corn

1 clove garlic

100 g coarse polenta

50 g freshly grated parmesan (preferably grana padano)

salt

1 To make the polenta, grate corn directly into a heavy-based saucepan. Peel and crush garlic and add to pan with 500 ml water. Bring to a boil over a moderate flame before 'raining' in polenta, stirring with a wooden spoon. Cover and reduce heat to a mere simmer and cook for 15 minutes. Remove lid and beat in parmesan. Season polenta well with salt, then pour directly onto your bench or a tray or similar to cool. Don't panic – the polenta will only end up about the size of a large dinner plate.

2 In a small frying pan, toast fennel seeds for several minutes, shaking the pan occasionally, until just golden, then grind to a powder in a mortar and pestle and set aside. Discard outer layer from each fennel bulb, then pick off feathery green tips and set aside. Slice each bulb into 4 pieces, ideally 1 cm thick.

3 Pour olive oil into a large baking dish or 2 smaller ones and arrange fennel in a single layer. Cook over a moderate flame to caramelise each side until deep golden. Peel and crush garlic, then add to fennel with tomato passata, wine, stock, lemon zest and juice, herbs and ground fennel seeds. Bring to a boil, then reduce to a simmer for 25 minutes until fennel is tender. Pick out thyme stalks, then add olives and fennel tips – if your olives are larger than the ones I use, you may like to let them warm through a little. (Alternatively, you can bake the fennel in the oven after the initial caramelisation. Drench scrunched up baking paper, then tuck this over the fennel to keep it submerged and bake at 175°C for around the same time, checking and shaking the dish after 15 minutes.)

4 While the fennel is simmering, cut cooled polenta into 4–6 wedges, brush with a little olive oil, and pan-fry or chargrill on both sides until deep golden and crisp. Taste fennel and adjust seasoning before serving with crisped polenta.

Just as the lively anise zing of a fennel bulb can be tamed and sweetened by a slow flame, the curry lift of the seeds is set free when roasted and ground.

Spring Soup

Weeding nettles has never been as sweet, each sting avenged all the more with this health-giving tonic in mind. If you don't have your own vegie patch, just head down to your local market and grab the freshest greens available. A good greengrocer should have green garlic and cavolo nero (also known as Tuscan kale), but if you can't find them you could try garlic and rocket instead. A small dollop of horseradish makes a lively substitute for the nettles, and the characteristic zing from the sorrel balances the sweetness of the peas, which in turn give body to the soup.

It's important to use a light chook stock here – a dark stock will tarnish the vibrancy of the green vegetables. Alternatively, if your stock is already made and a touch too dark, dilute it with water to brighten things up.

SERVES **4–6**

750 ml light Chook Stock (see page 191)

800 g peas in the pod

1 large handful flat-leaf parsley

3 leeks

3 heads green garlic

2 large (gloved!) handfuls nettles *or* 1 small horseradish root

2 large handfuls sorrel

2 large handfuls spinach

6 large cavolo nero leaves

100 ml olive oil

1 sprig thyme

1 handful mint leaves

salt

freshly ground black pepper

castor sugar (optional)

white-wine vinegar (optional)

extra-virgin olive oil (optional)

1 Put the stock into a saucepan, then shell peas and add pods to stock. Wash parsley, then pick leaves and add stalks to stock. Bring stock to a boil.

2 Meanwhile, prepare remaining greens. Cut away top quarter from leeks and garlic and discard, then cut remainder into 1 cm rounds. Wash well in a colander – submerge in water and rub away grit caught between layers – then drain. Wearing gloves, pick nettle leaves from stalks, then wash well and spin or shake dry and drain on paper towel. Trim stalks from sorrel, spinach and cavolo nero and wash similarly.

3 Heat olive oil over a moderate flame in a medium-sized heavy-based stockpot. Sweat leek and garlic for several minutes until tender, stirring frequently with a wooden spoon to avoid browning. Strain stock into pot, then add thyme and bring to a boil. Throw in three-quarters of the nettles, all the peas and cavolo nero, then lower heat and maintain a steady boil for about 5 minutes until peas are tender. Add parsley leaves and spinach and the minute the pot returns to a boil, remove from stove and allow to cool to room temperature.

4 Ladle cooled soup into a blender, removing thyme stalk as you go, then add sorrel and mint and blend for several minutes. Pass through a fine sieve or the fine blade of a Mouli, then season well. Depending on the sweetness of the peas, you may find a pinch or two of castor sugar helps enhance the flavour.

5 If you have not used nettles, purée finely grated horseradish with a drizzle of white-wine vinegar, a splash of extra-virgin olive oil and a few drops of boiling water with salt to taste. Reheat soup by bringing it just to a boil with saved nettle leaves or horseradish paste (add paste a little at a time, tasting as you go), then serve. If you like, you can fry nettle leaves in a little olive oil until crisp, then scatter over the soup before serving.

This deep emerald soup is a real spring vitamiser, more so if the greens are harvested from your own garden!

Chunky Gazpacho

The crunchy texture of this soup means there is (thankfully) no need to thicken it with soaked bread in the traditional Spanish manner. Instead, I scatter bits of crispy fried bread over the top and warm to the clean, glistening summery colours that an addition of bread would have sullied. Whether you prefer chilled gazpacho smooth, coarse or even slightly chunky like me, select full-flavoured, burstingly ripe tomatoes, such as oxhearts. This soup will jump right out of the bowl if you use the ripest vegetables, a top-quality aged vinegar and a freshly pressed, unfiltered extra-virgin olive oil.

SERVES **4–6**

5 small cucumbers

1 large red pepper

1 yellow pepper

1 large red onion

2 cloves garlic

500 g burstingly ripe tomatoes
  (preferably oxheart or beefsteak)

2 tablespoons Spanish sherry vinegar

salt

freshly ground black pepper

1 × 150 g piece crustless good bread

200 ml extra-virgin olive oil

2 sprigs thyme

1 handful mint leaves

1 handful basil leaves

1 Peel cucumbers and pass 3 through a juice extractor, seeds and all. Halve remaining cucumbers lengthways. Sit a fine-meshed strainer over a bowl, then scrape in seeds and push with back of a large spoon to extract all juices before discarding seed pulp. Finely dice cucumbers and add to juice.

2 Cut peppers in half and remove all seeds and cores. Using a vegetable peeler, peel skin from each pepper half, then finely dice flesh and add to cucumber. Dice onion finely and add to bowl with 1 minced garlic clove.

3 Peel, core and dice tomatoes (perhaps slightly larger than other vegetables), then add to bowl with all seeds and juice from chopping board. Mix in vinegar and season well. Cover with plastic film and refrigerate for several hours at least before serving for flavours to meld.

4 Ten minutes before serving, tear bread into tiny bite-sized pieces. Heat half the olive oil in a small frying pan over a moderate flame for a few seconds. Fry lightly crushed remaining garlic clove and bread, tossing frequently, until deep golden, then add thyme sprigs for a final few seconds. Discard garlic and thyme and drain crispy bread on paper towel and allow to cool to room temperature. Tear mint and basil leaves into tiny pieces, then mix through soup with remaining olive oil and ladle soup into bowls. Serve scattered with fried bread.

Soup with Three Lives

With the nip of autumn in the air and a sniffle under the nose, I've slid my favourite enamelled soup pot onto a full flame.

In with a slurp of olive oil, then I take to the chunk of speck from the bundle of leftovers in the Esky. Turning it side-on, I cut off the rind, leaving as much tasty fat as I can. About one-inch cubes'll do. I throw them in and hear a hungry hiss. I set to dice the onions so they can join the sizzle to reach a deep caramel.

Meanwhile to the carrots. I peel, quarter lengthways, and then roughly slice them, munching on a stick as an appetiser. A woody core in the parsnip gets added to the compost tub and, after peeling the gnarly bulb of celeriac, I opt for a more petite dice. Fluff near the heart of a fennel bulb gets plucked onto the bench before I dice on, perhaps a bit larger…

I can hear the caramel slowing as it grabs the speck and onion closer to the bottom of the pot. Now's the time to rub with my wooden spoon – I'm salivating already at the sight of those sugary blobs. I grab a plastic bucket half filled with chook stock (from a previous life) and quickly scrape the congealed fat off the jellied surface, then in she goes.

By this stage my beagles are going crazy!

Off with ends of a few Brussels sprouts. I pull the greenest leaves onto the bench and thinly slice their hearts. An upright cob of corn falls to bits as my knife slides down the sides. Half a head of cauliflower gets plucked 'love-me-not' style, floret by floret – I save the stems for the chooks.

With the pot now up to a rolling boil, I grab a few last-of-season oxheart tomatoes. After a quick wipe, I plunge all three into the brew with not even a criss-cross. In half a minute they're out, dunked into cold water and with a wrinkle and a gentleman's stroke the skins slip off, then the knife does its thing. A juicy slop of seeds reminds me to scrape a few onto some paper towel for the next season's planting. Another cowboy-style rough dice, then in they go.

Now I'm in a bit of predicament with the potatoes. You see, I've got this friend visiting tomorrow and have visions of serving a clear broth alive with vitamins of every colour and shape. By then, spuds could turn things a bit murky. I'm reassured by the sight of a horseradish root and a few broad beans, so selfishly dice the spuds and throw 'em in.

All this enthusiasm has got my pot swelling dangerously close to the top, so before things get messy, I half submerge that bucket and bail out some of the excess broth (I may be needing that as those spuds mash themselves).

It's time for some aromatics. I duck outside to tear off a few sage leaves, sprigs of thyme and a bay leaf. The sprigs go in stalks and all, then I pound the sage leaves with a couple of garlic cloves in a mortar and pestle. (For a moment, I remember someone once warning me about using a bay leaf straight from the tree before I toss it in.) With the cured speck in mind I hold off on salt, then slide the pot onto the simmer side of the stove.

And now my spell is cast.

This is a blissful hour or two that in my restaurant

life would be bombarded with other tightly scheduled preparations. A slow simmer in weekend mode gives a whole treasured freedom – the luxury of time.

A lazy hour or so has slipped by and now the whole shack is thick with a seductive, sweet, smoky aroma. As I ladle the steaming brew, I pull out the bare twigs of thyme poking from our bowls, scatter over a coarse grating of parmesan, drizzle with a favourite Aussie extra-virgin and add a few twists of pepper – and we slurp on, ecstatically.

Later, before bedding down, there's a dark moment when I picture waking to an over-reduced crust, so I refill the pot with our saved broth, slide on the lid and tuck a simmer mat underneath.

We wake the next day permeated by the brew. With fresh enthusiasm, each broad bean gets a snap and pop from their pods for a quick blanch in some boiling salted water followed by a cooling dunk. With a flick and a squeeze the inner lime green buttons slide out from their bitter skins. An eruption from the beagles lets me know our guest has arrived.

Together we tear a few leaves of spinach from the garden and head down the path. Before we reach the door, my wafting aroma hits and I grin like the proverbial Cheshire cat. 'It's been simmering all night!' I brag (with a certain conceit), and then set to freshen things up. In go those broad beans and spinach leaves. Yesterday's bread is toasted and rubbed with garlic and a fine grating of that old horseradish root lifts the brew up from the grave.

Come late afternoon, I chill the refilled bucket down for our trip back to the coast and its final resurrection. By now my soggy vegetables have totally surrendered every flavour into the broth. With a blast of modern trickery, I've poured the remnants into a blender. My final deception – much to Plato's disgrace – is all silken and smooth. I'm aglow with a warm feeling of achievement, having fuelled and fooled with a thrifty use of leftovers spanning three days.

I returned home from the restaurant late that evening to find the bucket empty in the sink, a sight that tickles a private g-spot in any caring cook – all finished!

Roasted Red Pepper Soup

This cooling summer soup came about when I puréed a few leftover roasted and peeled red peppers with a pan of sautéed onion and some stock. Now I roast everything together and deglaze the baking dish to collect all the natural sugars. I like to serve this velvety, rust-coloured soup with a dollop of sheep's milk yoghurt and a sprinkling of mint.

SERVES **4–6**

5 red peppers

2 large onions

½ head garlic

1 bird's-eye chilli (optional)

3 sprigs thyme

175 ml olive oil

salt

freshly ground black pepper

250 ml Chook Stock (see page 191)

250 ml dry white wine

1 tablespoon balsamic vinegar

1 × 100 g piece crustless good bread

125 g sheep's milk yoghurt (preferably Meredith)

1 handful mint leaves

1   Preheat oven to 180°C. Cut peppers in half and remove tops, seeds and cores, then arrange in one layer in a large baking dish (you may need to use 2). Peel onions and cut into rough 3 cm chunks, then add to peppers. Peel garlic and add all but 1 clove to dish with chilli, if using, and 2 of the thyme sprigs, then rub vegetables well with 125 ml of the olive oil and season well. Cover with foil and roast for 1 hour– 1 hour 20 minutes until deeply caramelised, moving vegetables with a wooden spoon every 20 minutes or so to avoid catching.

2   Stand baking dish over a moderate flame and deglaze with stock, wine and vinegar and allow to boil up for several minutes, rubbing the base of the dish constantly with your wooden spoon to loosen all the goodies. Remove from heat and leave to cool to room temperature. Purée cooled roasted vegetables and their juices in a blender, then pass purée through a fine sieve or the fine blade of a Mouli. Taste for seasoning and adjust, if necessary, then refrigerate until chilled.

3   Ten minutes before serving, tear bread into tiny bite-sized pieces. Heat remaining olive oil in a small frying pan over a moderate flame for a few seconds. Fry lightly crushed remaining garlic clove and bread, tossing frequently, until deep golden, then add saved thyme sprig for a final few seconds. Discard garlic and thyme and drain crispy bread on paper towel and allow to cool to room temperature.

4   Ladle the cool soup into bowls, then dollop on some yoghurt and scatter with fried bread and torn mint leaves.

Borscht from Belarus

I've always been slightly confused by borscht – there are dozens of different recipes for this deep-red beetroot soup from Russia, Lithuania and the Ukraine (even green versions made with sorrel) and they can be served hot or cold. And then I was invited to the Joffe family's table. The Joffes are from Polotsk in the Republic of Belarus, and their chilled soup is laden with chopped scarlet-stained egg, cucumber, spring onions and dill, and they serve steaming boiled potatoes on the side. Apart from swapping tinned beets for fresh, this recipe is a tribute to sharing their family tradition.

SERVES **4–6**
800 g beetroot
salt
3 large eggs
2 small cucumbers
1 generous handful dill
4 spring onions
200 g sour cream
1 tablespoon red-wine vinegar
freshly ground black pepper
a little castor sugar (optional)
4–6 smallish waxy potatoes (preferably kipfler)

1   Remove leaves from beets with a twist (save these for sautéeing and tossing through pasta, if you like). Put half the beets into a small saucepan, then cover with cold water and add a large pinch of salt. Boil beets until just tender when tested with a fork or skewer. Refresh under cool water, then rub off skins.

2   Meanwhile, peel remaining beets with a vegetable peeler and pass through a juicer. Skim scum from surface before pouring juice into a large, preferably stainless-steel bowl (this aids a quicker chill). Chop cooked beets into 5 mm dice and add to juice (the soup base).

3   Put eggs into a small saucepan, then cover with warm water and bring to a boil. Cook for 5 minutes (the yolks should be just firm). Cool eggs under running water, then peel and chop roughly into 5 mm dice and add to soup.

4   Peel cucumbers, then halve lengthways and scoop seeds into a fine-meshed strainer set directly over beetroot juice mixture. Push on seeds with back of a large spoon to extract all juices. Cut cucumber into 5 mm dice. Pick dill leaves from stalks, then coarsely chop, and peel and finely slice spring onions. Add these ingredients to soup too.

5   Stir sour cream into soup with vinegar, then season well with salt and pepper. Add a little castor sugar to enhance the flavours, if you like. Cover and refrigerate for at least 1 hour (several, ideally).

6   Shortly before you plan to eat, boil potatoes, then peel. Serve the chilled borscht in wide, shallow bowls with a steaming boiled potato in the middle of each (or on the side, like the Joffes, if you prefer) and a ceremonial shot of frosty Russian vodka alongside.

The borscht ceremony, of course, begins with the chink of glasses and a riveting shot of the best Russian vodka.

Asparagus with Pine-nut Mayonnaise

In the mid-1980s Martin Teplitzky, of Bon Cafard restaurant in Darlinghurst, seduced many, including me, with his steamed asparagus masked with heavenly, warm pine-nut mayonnaise. At the time, most restaurants were serving asparagus with hollandaise or lemon butter. The combination of the slightly sweet nuttiness of the roasted pine nuts and the clean, earthy juice bursting from the spears is utterly delightful.

Using a whole egg lifts and lightens this mayonnaise as it cooks and thickens slightly when the pine nuts and oil are added hot from the pan. The mayonnaise keeps well, refrigerated, although I prefer to serve it freshly made at room temperature.

While thin spears of asparagus need no peeling, I find the more robustly flavoured fat spears tend to have tough skin towards their base that needs to be removed.

SERVES **4–6**

30–40 asparagus spears
salt
2 cloves garlic
2 egg yolks
1 egg
50 ml white-wine vinegar
juice of 1 lemon
375 ml olive oil
100 g pine nuts
50 ml boiling water
freshly ground black pepper

1   Snap each asparagus spear towards base to separate fibrous from tender part of stalk. Carefully peel about a quarter of the way up spear. Fill a deep, wide pan or asparagus steamer with cold water and add a generous pinch of salt, then bring to a boil.

2   Meanwhile, make the mayonnaise. Peel and roughly crush garlic cloves. Whiz 1 garlic clove, yolks, egg, vinegar, lemon juice and a generous sprinkling of salt in a food processor until smooth, then very slowly drizzle in half the olive oil while the motor is still running. Leave mayonnaise in food processor.

3   Plunge asparagus into the boiling water and cook for 4–5 minutes until tender, then drain thoroughly. While asparagus is boiling, cook pine nuts and remaining garlic clove in other half of olive oil in a frying pan over a moderate flame until deep golden, stirring occasionally and watching carefully to ensure nuts don't burn. Using a large spoon, add nuts and oil to mayonnaise and whiz again, but avoid over-puréeing (a slightly grainy texture is preferred). Drizzle in boiling water, pulsing motor as you go. Season mayonnaise to taste. Divide asparagus between plates and mask with warm mayonnaise, or serve the two separately, if eating with your fingers (but no double-dipping!).

I always choose turgid, deep-green asparagus that show no signs of seeding at the tips.

Brussels Sprouts Sautéed with Garlic and Sage

There is something deeply comforting about leftovers politely bubble'n'squeaking in a pan. I could tell Mum was proud of hers. The previous night (or the night before that) she would've served us the dreaded Brussels sprouts. Like most mums, ours boiled the life out of 'em – a depressing mush in the mouth none of us could finish, waterlogged and always tasting strangely metallic. Her desperate claims that they'd put hairs on our chests only amused us, especially with my sister at the table, so naturally they always made it into the squeak.

We could usually identify potato, pumpkin, sometimes carrot, onion and lamb bits all bound by leftover Gravox. I remember thinking the bubble'n'squeak was getting a bit too fancy when I found choko (the back fence was covered in them) but enjoyed it nonetheless. Cabbage rarely made an appearance, however. Thankfully Mum gave up shredding and boiling, adopting a stir-fry method. The leaves were slippery, a little crunchy and naturally sweet, so there was never any left.

But what bubble'n'squeak did to Mum's Brussels sprouts was revolutionary. Not only were they hugged by a delicious, slightly sweet and salty crust, but they were finally rid of all the water and devoured with new enthusiasm, then we'd all be happily off to do a little bubble'n'squeaking ourselves . . .

I now take to Brussels sprouts the way Mum took to cabbage. For added interest I sometimes add a few leaves of cavolo nero (that black cabbage also known as Tuscan kale), along with ground cumin and diced bacon or pancetta. I serve the sprouts alongside a roasted game bird such as pheasant or guinea fowl, but I can just as easily eat them on their own.

6 Brussels sprouts per person
duck fat *or* **olive oil**
garlic cloves
sage leaves
salt
freshly ground black pepper

1   Cut a thin slice away from base of each sprout to help free the greenest leaves until you reach the pale, tight heart. Slice trimmed sprouts thinly.

2   Melt a dollop of duck fat in a suitably sized frying pan (or line it with olive oil). Finely mince a clove or two of garlic with a few sage leaves, then sauté sprouts, garlic and sage over a moderate flame for several minutes until tender. Season to taste before serving.

Flowering Zucchini Stuffed with Mozzarella, Basil and Anchovy, and Deep-fried

If you are lucky enough to have a rambling zucchini growing in your garden, I suggest preparing your stuffing before skipping out to the open flowers waiting hungrily in the sun. Gently flick out the stamens, feed each flower with a mozzarella 'sandwich', then twist the petals closed and snap each blossom free from the plant. Back in the real world, ask your greengrocer for about three flowers per person – in both cases, be sure to wipe any grit off with a damp cloth.

The addition of ice cubes to the batter increases the temperature difference with the hot oil, causing the batter to bubble-up and become extra light and airy.

SERVES **6**

1 generous handful basil

2 cloves garlic

salt

500 g mozzarella

6 large anchovies

18 flowering zucchini (courgettes)

4 litres sunflower oil

freshly ground black pepper

lemon wedges

BATTER

1 × 330 ml stubby of beer

150 g plain flour

150 g ice-cubes

1 teaspoon salt

1   Strip leaves from basil and peel garlic. In a mortar and pestle, pound basil and garlic to a coarse paste with a sprinkling of salt. Cut mozzarella into 36 pieces about 2 cm long × 1 cm wide × 5 mm thick. Cut anchovies into thirds. Put a piece of anchovy on 18 pieces of cheese. Dollop basil paste evenly over each anchovy, then sandwich with remaining cheese. Wipe any grit from outside of flowers, then carefully open and remove stamens before sliding in cheese 'sandwich' as far as possible. Gently twist petals together, then lay stuffed flowers on a tray with twisted petals supported up against the side.

2   To make the batter, mix all ingredients roughly with a spoon to make a lumpy batter (aim for lumps the size of grains of rice). Leave to sit for several minutes until spoon is left with a thin coating when lifted above bowl.

3   Preheat oven to 150°C. Meanwhile, preheat sunflower oil to 180°C in a deep-fryer or a heavy-based pan large enough to hold double the volume (the oil will bubble up during cooking). Prepare to cook zucchini flowers in batches of 6. Hold a flower at each end, keeping petals twisted, and immerse in batter. Drain excess before gently floating in hot oil and frying for several minutes, turning carefully with tongs, until deep golden. Drain on paper towel, then keep warm in oven (or stand around in the kitchen and eat them as you go!). Season and serve hot with lemon wedges.

Choose pert female flowers for this dish – these are the ones attached to the zucchini. Stuffed and fried, the edible stem in hand gives a welcome burst of young zucchini juice.

Broad Bean Salad with Shaved Fennel, Pear and Pecorino

The broad or 'fava' bean makes the most handsome addition to a vegetable patch, with its dark-eyed cream flowers and oceanic bluey-green leaves. I can't resist a healthy pile of the young beans, quickly blanched then devoured, pods and all. While some people pod broad beans and then painstakingly peel every single bean, I only peel the bitter skins away from any slightly larger beans, the vibrant lime green of these naked beauties an appealing contrast to their tiny, tender sage-green brothers. Older beans are best made into a purée, as they become 'mealy'. I have even added the velvety, emptied pods to a pot of potatoes in a thrifty moment, the resulting purée enhanced by a slightly beany flavour.

This lively, crunchy salad is slightly sweet with pear and balanced by the grassy saltiness of sheep's milk cheese, be it pecorino, an aged sheep's cheese from the New South Wales Riverina region or a paler, softer fetta, from Victoria's Meredith Dairy, for example.

SERVES **4**

2 kg broad beans in the pod
salt
150 ml extra-virgin olive oil
finely grated zest and juice of 1 lemon
freshly ground black pepper
½ teaspoon castor sugar (optional)
120 g pecorino
2 small bulbs fennel
2 just-ripe pears (preferably Josephine
   or Doyenné du comice)
a few mint leaves

1 Pop broad beans from their pods and blanch in boiling salted water for about 20 seconds, then swiftly refresh in iced water until cool. Drain beans and carefully nick outer skin of largest beans, then squeeze out beans. Leave smallest beans as they are.

2 Whisk extra-virgin olive oil into lemon juice in a small bowl, then add lemon zest and season to taste. Adjust acidity with castor sugar, if you like.

3 Shave pecorino – I use a mandoline for this. Trim and discard outer layer from fennel bulbs, saving a few young, tender green tips. Slice fennel very thinly lengthways, removing core as you go. Peel and quarter pears, then slice very thinly lengthways. Tear mint leaves and toss gently in a large mixing bowl with fennel, pear, beans and enough dressing to coat lightly, then season and toss gently again. Arrange salad on plates, layering with pecorino, and serve at once, drizzled with remaining dressing.

Tomato Hand-me-downs

At an heirloom-tomato tasting a few years back at 'Heronswood', home of The Digger's Club (see page 189), in Dromana, Victoria, I was bowled over by the array. These were exotic fruit of extraordinary hues, from glowing golden to charcoal, from the zebra to the Mexican midget (which sprang like a flea as it burst in my mouth). It was incredible to think that the only reason these tomatoes are available today is that their seeds have been handed from generation to generation for centuries, saved each season by gardeners for their longer cropping (thanks to a higher resistance to pests) and superior flavour.

For me, the epitome of summer comes in the form of the irregular, bulbous oxheart tomato, burstingly ripe and eaten blood-warm, as Mother Nature intended. The oxheart is unrivalled for its gob-stopping meatiness and is largely the cause of my insatiable lust for full-flavoured, old-fashioned, field-grown tomatoes.

From the time I first started venturing to Sydney's Flemington markets almost twenty years ago until the time of writing, there has remained a solitary, devoted oxheart grower in the local shed. Perhaps out of supermarket aspirations, a few hybridised oxheart/roma impostors have emerged. The true heirloom remains loyal to its heritage and is snubbed by supermarkets, mainly because it won't stack. Now, if supermarket fare was selected on flavour alone . . .

My favourite way to serve oxhearts is in the Italian caprese manner, with fresh, soft mozzarella, basil and plenty of fruity extra-virgin olive oil. To maximise sensuality I reckon it's essential to cut the tomato into chunks large enough to fill the mouth.

Make a dressing by pounding a generous handful of basil leaves, a clove of garlic and a sprinkling of salt in a mortar and pestle (or pulse in a blender). Pour in just enough extra-virgin to make it loose and pesto-like.

Lightly crush several large, meaty olives just enough to slip out the pips. Arrange the tomato chunks on a serving platter, then drizzle sparingly with well-aged balsamic vinegar and season with salt flakes and freshly ground black pepper. Mask the tomato with the basil dressing, then tuck in pieces of mozzarella, torn to the same size as the chunks (or choose 'nodine', knots of mozzarella, if you come across them), and stop the gaps with the olives. Tear a few contrasting purple basil leaves over the top, then glaze the lot with your best extra-virgin olive oil and serve with crusty bread.

Alternatively, if you can get hold of fresh mozzarella made with buffalo milk, try serving it torn into rough pieces and scattered over a thickly sliced oxheart 'steak'. Dress this with anchovies melted in the hot, nutty oil that has just fried several cloves of crushed garlic.

If you can't be bothered, devour your tomato privately, just as it is, perhaps with a sprinkling of salt flakes, and I guarantee you'll be hooked for life.

Goat's Cheese Salad with Golden Beets, Blood Orange and Radishes

This lively salad makes an ideal lunch and is a colourful celebration of spring.

SERVES 4–6

6 golfball-sized golden beetroot
150 g crustless good bread
200 ml extra-virgin olive oil
1 clove garlic
4 sprigs thyme
1 romano *or* other bitter green lettuce
6 radishes
1 generous handful chives
4 blood oranges
2 tablespoons walnut oil
2 tablespoons sherry vinegar
1 teaspoon castor sugar
3 heads red witlof *or* radicchio
1 × 250 g log fresh goat's cheese
salt
freshly ground black pepper

1   Preheat oven to 200°C. Twist each beet from its stalk, saving a few of the tiniest leaves but discarding the rest, then wash and pat dry. Wrap each beet in foil and bake for 25–35 minutes until just tender when tested with a metal skewer or cook's fork. Unwrap beets and leave to cool to room temperature before rubbing off skins.

2   Meanwhile, tear bread into tiny bite-sized pieces. Heat half the extra-virgin olive oil in a frying pan over a moderate flame for a few seconds. Fry lightly crushed garlic clove and bread, tossing frequently, until deep golden, then add thyme sprigs for a final few seconds. Drain crispy bread on paper towel and allow to cool to room temperature.

3   Discard all outer leaves from lettuce, retaining just the tender hearts, then wash and dry. Trim radishes about 1 cm above tops, then rinse well and thinly slice from top to bottom and tip into a large bowl. Finely chop chives and add to bowl.

4   Segment blood oranges by slicing off just enough from tops and bottoms to reveal inner flesh. Using a small, sharp knife and cutting down orange, cut skin and pith away in strips. Holding orange over a small bowl, carefully cut segments free by sliding your knife down either side of connective tissue. When you're finished, give remnants a final squeeze into bowl before discarding. Add orange segments to radishes. Make a dressing by whisking juice from orange segments with remaining extra-virgin olive oil, walnut oil, vinegar and sugar, then add salt to taste.

5   Remove outer witlof leaves to reveal hearts. Cut each outer leaf into 3 bite-sized pieces, then add to bowl with hearts (trimmed of excess core), lettuce and saved beet leaves. Tear goat's cheese into rough 1 cm cubes, then toss gently through salad with salt, pepper, dressing and fried bread and arrange loosely in serving bowls.

Globe Artichokes Simmered in Olive Oil with Gremolata and Toasted Crumbs

A true artichoke aficionado, my Tuscan friend Sebastiano revels at being handed a whole thistle snapped straight off the bush and is the one who introduced me to this treat. The ceremony novel to me, I soon caught on as we dipped each leaf into a bowl of fruity olive oil and scraped the slightly sweet and nutty flesh from each leaf. I've since realised that growing your own is the key to this delicacy, ensuring the artichokes are 'squeaking' fresh.

If you don't grow your own, try simmering bought artichokes in a dressing and serve them loosely stuffed with herbs and toasted crumbs. Goat's cheese adds an interesting complexity, although might be considered a bastardisation in the eyes of someone like Sebastiano.

SERVES 4–6

1 litre extra-virgin olive oil
6 cloves garlic
several oregano leaves
several sage leaves
several sprigs thyme
150 ml dry white wine
2 lemons
4–6 globe artichokes
salt
freshly ground black pepper
1 handful coarse fresh breadcrumbs
2 handfuls flat-leaf parsley leaves

1   Pour oil into a lidded enamelled cast-iron pot into which artichokes will fit snugly. Peel and coarsely smash 4 of the garlic cloves, then roughly chop oregano and sage leaves and add to oil with thyme and wine. Zest and juice 1 lemon and add to pot.

2   Trim about 3 cm from top of each artichoke, then cut away (but keep) stalks so flowers will sit flat. Discard a few darker outside leaves and tidy up any fibres with a sharp knife, then submerge in oil. Carefully peel each stalk to its paler centre, keeping it smooth and as round as possible. Add these to oil as well and season generously.

3   Bring pot to a boil over a moderate flame, then reduce to a steady simmer until stalks are just tender, about 25 minutes. Remove stalks with a slotted spoon and leave to cool. Return pot to heat and simmer until hearts are tender, about another 25 minutes. Remove with a slotted spoon and allow to cool. Keep cooking juices in pot – these become the dressing later on.

4   Add a spoonful of oil from the very top of the artichoke pot (avoiding liquids at bottom) to a frying pan and heat over a moderate flame, then sauté breadcrumbs until deep golden. Drain on paper towel. Meanwhile, make the gremolata by removing zest from remaining lemon and mincing it with remaining garlic cloves and parsley.

5   When artichokes are cool enough to handle, carefully part centre leaves to reveal the fibrous, furry 'choke'. Carefully scoop this out using a teaspoon and discard. Open up flower and loosely stuff gremolata and crumbs between leaves and in heart. Stir cooking juices well and check seasoning, then drizzle generously over artichoke hearts and stalks and serve.

Silk Aubergines Roasted with Mozzarella, Tomato and Anchovy

In this instance, we're talking about a silk aubergine, not your coal-coloured, down-the-shops eggplant. They have fewer seeds than their darker cousins and much creamier flesh. Late summer and through autumn is their season, usually the same time as tomatoes are at their best. Choose the more rounded specimens for serving individually, ideally about the size of your clenched fist. As the skin tends to shrink and toughen with cooking, I like to peel it zebra-striped, so the eggplants can show off their most vibrant hues with just enough skin for structural support.

SERVES 6

6 silk aubergines

salt

500 g burstingly ripe tomatoes

freshly ground black pepper

1 pinch castor sugar

3 cloves garlic

1 sprig thyme

100 ml olive oil

6 green basil leaves

1 tablespoon balsamic vinegar

3 litres sunflower or olive oil

6 handfuls rocket

6 golfball-sized pieces mozzarella

6 plump anchovies

12 purple basil leaves

DIJON MUSTARD DRESSING

1 clove garlic

1 teaspoon Dijon mustard

1 teaspoon white-wine vinegar

100 ml extra-virgin olive oil

salt

freshly ground black pepper

1   Using a vegetable peeler or small, sharp knife and working from top to bottom, cut away 2 cm wide strips of aubergine skin to leave a zebra-striped pattern of flesh and skin. Cut stem-ends away and trim bases a little. Using a small, sharp knife, cut deeply into exposed flesh at top of each aubergine, leaving a 1 cm 'lip'. Cut all the way around – avoid piercing sides. Slash centre, then scoop out seeds, being careful not to break through base. Sprinkle cavity with salt (don't overdo this – just as if seasoning) and leave to sweat for about 1 hour.

2   Meanwhile, preheat oven to 200°C. Cut tomatoes in half and arrange in a baking dish, then season well with salt, pepper and sugar. Peel and coarsely smash garlic, then scatter over tomato with thyme. Drizzle with olive oil and roast for 15–20 minutes until deep golden. Add green basil, then slightly crush tomato with a wooden spoon and drizzle with vinegar. Return to oven for a further 5 minutes. Stir tomato vigorously with a wooden spoon to gather all caramelised juices, then pass through a sieve or coarse blade of a Mouli (to remove tomato seeds) before puréeing in a blender. Set aside. Leave oven on.

The freshest silk aubergines look almost regal, swathed in their glossed cream and purple cloaks.

3 Preheat sunflower or olive oil to 180°C in a deep-fryer or a heavy-based pan large enough to hold double the volume (the oil will bubble up during cooking). Dry aubergines thoroughly inside and out with paper towel before deep-frying to golden brown, rolling them around and gently holding them under the oil with a wooden spoon so they colour evenly. Remove with a slotted spoon and drain on paper towel.

4 Wash and dry rocket, discarding any yellowing leaves. To make the Dijon mustard dressing, peel and lightly crush garlic clove, then whisk it in a small bowl with mustard, vinegar and extra-virgin olive oil. Season to taste.

5 Cut each piece of mozzarella in half, then tuck a piece into each aubergine cavity, followed by 2 spoonfuls tomato sauce, another piece of mozzarella and finally an anchovy. Bake stuffed aubergines for 8–10 minutes, then serve on a bed of rocket tossed with torn purple basil leaves and mustard dressing.

White Bean Soup with Pipis and Chorizo

For this comforting yet surprisingly light Portuguese-style soup, use fresh borlotti beans in season or dried Lima beans (just remember to allow time to soak the dried beans overnight). Chorizo brings vitality and smokiness to the pot, balancing the sweetness of the caramelised onion and celeriac. Once the pipis burst open in response to the heat, the beans snuggle neatly into the butterflied purple shells as the flavour of the sea floods the dish.

Depending on where you live, you may know pipis as something else. For me, a pipi has always had a smooth shell, while a clam (or cockle), a ridged one. To confuse things further, my fishmonger and I always refer to those tiny, purple-blushed clams as 'vongole'. Does it matter really since they all 'clam' when they need to?! Choose whatever takes your fancy on the day.

It's not really necessary to use a Mouli or blender here, as I've suggested, but the result will be silkier and creamier if you do. You could also use a hand-held blender, but you'll need to strain the soup to remove the celeriac fibres and tiny bits of bean skin.

SERVES 4–6

1 kg fresh borlotti beans in the pod
   or 150 g dried Lima beans
1 kg pipis
3 large onions
1 celeriac
3 cloves garlic
75 ml olive oil
150 ml dry white wine
750 ml Fish Stock (see page 192)
finely grated zest of 1 lemon
several sprigs of thyme
1 handful flat-leaf parsley
150 g mild *or* hot chorizo
salt
freshly ground black pepper

1   If using dried Lima beans, soak them overnight in four times their volume of cold water. Next day, drain off soaking water and add clean water to four times the volume of beans again and bring to a boil. Lower heat to a simmer and cook for at least 1 hour, tasting along the way, until tender, then drain.

2   Meanwhile, rinse pipis under a running tap, then tip into a bucket and cover with clean water. Leave to purge of sand for several hours.

3   When you are ready to start making the soup, pod borlotti beans, if using, then boil in plenty of unsalted water (adding salt when cooking legumes tends to toughen skins) until tender, 30–40 minutes. Set aside a couple of handfuls of whole and plump beans, whether borlotti or Lima.

4   Peel and roughly dice onions and celeriac, then peel and smash garlic cloves. Heat oil in a medium-sized, heavy-based pan over a low flame, then add onion, celeriac and garlic and sweat gently for about 20 minutes, stirring occasionally to avoid browning. Add wine, stock, lemon zest and majority of beans and bring to a boil. Reduce heat and simmer for 30 minutes. Remove pan from stove and allow to cool slightly. Pass soup base through a Mouli or sieve, then purée in a blender until smooth. Rinse out pan.

5   Ten minutes before serving, pick thyme leaves from stalks. Wash parsley and tear off leaves, then set aside. Drain pipis. If chorizo is soft, cut in half lengthways and scrape flesh from skin, then crumble into bite-sized pieces. (If it's not soft, just dice sausage instead.) Heat rinsed-out pan over a moderate flame and throw in sausage for a couple of minutes to lightly caramelise, giving the pot a shake, then add thyme, pipis and soup base. Bring to a boil and allow to boil steadily for several minutes, stirring occasionally until pipis start to pop open, then add saved beans and parsley. When every pipi has opened, correct seasoning with salt and pepper. Serve in warm wide bowls with a shell-dumping bowl on the side.

Prawn Chowder

Unlike the famed American Boston or Manhattan chowders, ours at Sean's Panaroma is made without tomato or cream and always with corn. I find tomato acid wrestles with the natural sugars in the corn and tarnishes its golden hue. And instead of cream I prefer to use olive oil for gloss (and health).

Some chowders are enhanced by sautéed diced bacon or speck. Whatever your preference, aim for a silky-smooth consistency – here, the added texture comes from a dice of potato, a few corn kernels and tender prawns. Try the Chinese 'velveting' technique below when preparing the prawns, to avoid any characteristic toughening – this massaging tradition tenderises the flesh remarkably.

SERVES 4–6

500 g green king prawns
¼ cup cornflour
1 teaspoon bicarbonate of soda
⅓ teaspoon cumin seeds
2 large onions
3 cobs best corn
⅓ cup olive oil
100 ml dry white wine
1.5 litres Prawn Stock (see page 193)
½ head garlic
⅓ cup Chilli Oil (see page 195)
1 handful basil leaves
2 smallish new-season waxy potatoes (preferably kipfler)
1 pinch saffron threads
salt
freshly ground black pepper
2 spring onions
extra-virgin olive oil

1   Peel and devein prawns (save shells for making stock), then cut into bite-sized chunks. 'Velvet' prawnmeat by massaging it with cornflour and bicarbonate of soda for 2–3 minutes. Transfer prawnmeat to a colander and massage under cold running water for another 5 minutes. Drain well, then refrigerate, covered, until needed.

2   In a small dry frying pan, toast cumin seeds over a low flame until fragrant, then cool and grind. Peel and roughly chop onions. Remove ears and silk from corn, then cut kernels from cobs. Heat olive oil over a moderate flame in a heavy-based pan, then add onion and sauté until lightly caramelised. Add ground cumin and sauté for another few minutes until fragrant. Add corn (keeping a handful or two aside for later) and sauté briefly to lightly caramelise sugars oozing from kernels. Deglaze pan with wine, then add stock and bring to a boil. Meanwhile, peel and roughly crush garlic cloves and add to pot with chilli oil, then reduce heat and simmer for about 40 minutes. Add basil to pan, then pour soup base through a strainer set over a large bowl or bucket. Purée solids left in strainer in a blender with just enough strained liquid to keep it all moving, then pass purée through a Mouli or sieve back into remaining liquid.

3   Ten minutes before serving, peel and dice potatoes. Return soup base to pan, then add potato, saffron and saved corn kernels, then bring to a simmer over a moderate flame. When potato is tender, add 'velveted' prawns and cook until just pink – this will only take a minute or so. Season with salt and pepper and skim away any scum. Ladle into heated bowls, then sprinkle with finely sliced spring onion and drizzle with extra-virgin olive oil to serve.

Prawn Broth with Prawn and Cauliflower Dumplings

Made using a technique similar to the French process of binding fish with egg white and cream, these light, slightly sweet dumplings have a rather radical texture. Floating in clear, steaming broth, they are studded with chopped prawns and cauliflower, their irregularity making them all the more charming.

Don't be alarmed by having to add egg whites to the broth. As the broth cooks, the egg whites congeal, trapping with them all solids and impurities. This 'raft' is simply lifted out and – hey presto – below lies the sparkling clarified broth. Magic.

SERVES 4–6

500 g green prawns

1 large onion

1 large carrot

2 sticks celery

1 small bulb fennel

⅓ cup olive oil

2 cloves garlic

4 egg whites

2 ripe tomatoes

6 stalks parsley

1 bay leaf

2 sprigs thyme

5 peppercorns

finely grated zest of 1 orange

1 teaspoon castor sugar

salt

extra-virgin olive oil

DUMPLINGS

1 spring onion

100 g cauliflower

1 clove garlic

1 egg white

175 ml cream

1 teaspoon salt

1   Peel prawns, saving meat for dumplings and keeping shells and heads for broth. To make the broth, peel and roughly dice onion and carrot. Strip and discard leaves from celery and fennel, then roughly chop. Heat olive oil over a moderate flame in a large heavy-based pan, then sauté onion until lightly caramelised, stirring regularly. Whiz fennel, celery, carrot, prawn shells and peeled garlic with egg whites in a food processor for a couple of minutes to form a coarse paste. Roughly chop tomatoes and add to onion with paste. Pour in 2 litres water, then add herbs, peppercorns, orange zest and sugar. Bring to a boil, then lower heat and simmer for 30 minutes. Do not stir, otherwise you'll disturb egg-white 'raft'. Remove raft and gently ladle broth through a fine-meshed strainer lined with muslin, then season to taste with salt.

2   To make the dumplings, trim and finely slice spring onion and break cauliflower into tiny bite-sized florets (about 1 cm tall). Heat a little prawn broth in a small saucepan and blanch cauliflower for a minute or so until just tender, then remove to drain and cool. Strain broth and return it to main portion. Whiz garlic, egg white and three-quarters of the reserved prawn meat in a food processor for several minutes to form a paste, then tip into a bowl and fold in cream, salt and spring onion. Roughly chop remaining prawn meat and add to dumpling mixture with drained cauliflower. Cover with plastic film and refrigerate until you are about to eat.

3 Just before serving, bring broth to a boil over a high flame. When hot, ladle a cup of broth into a smaller pan over a low flame. Using 2 teaspoons, scoop 'mouthfuls' of dumpling mixture into the smaller pan. Simmer dumplings gently for 3 minutes until firm and cooked, then divide them between warmed bowls using a slotted spoon. Ensure the main broth is boiling before ladling it over the dumplings, then drizzle with a little extra-virgin olive oil and serve.

Abalone Seared with Green Garlic and Fennel

It's an understatement to say that live abalone is a delicacy. Scarcity, expense, yield and fine flavour have all added to its allure, and the fact that skilled preparation is required only heightens expectations. (Once the abalone is gutted and trimmed, it's all down to knife skills, so ensure you are sharp-edged and prepare to be patient!) But the future is looking brighter, now that the successful aquaculture of abalone has begun in Tasmania, South Australia and Victoria. With luck, this will mean more on the market, so more of us will have the chance to enjoy this treat.

When it comes to cooking abalone, whether green- or black-lipped, there are basically two options: a slow simmer or a fast sear. I particularly like the latter and the slight crunch and lift provided by the shaved fennel and young green garlic in the following dish, although would be more than thrilled if served abalone simply seared and unadorned. Alternatively, you can simmer scrubbed and trimmed whole abalone with olive oil and herbs for several hours (as you would a giant octopus) for a remarkably contrasting texture. This can then be sliced thinly when cool and served 'carpaccio' style, perhaps with a scattering of fried capers.

SERVES 2

1 live black- or green-lipped abalone
1 bulb baby fennel
1 head green garlic
1 handful basil leaves
100 ml extra-virgin olive oil
2–3 leaves iceberg lettuce
50 ml olive oil
salt
freshly ground black pepper
¼ lemon

1 Hold abalone 'ear' in palm of your hand. Using a large spoon, scoop out flesh, twisting spoon around edge of shell as you dig persuasively, staying in constant contact with inside of shell. Scrape away brown mucous attached to meat, then scrub off coloured membrane covering muscle with a stiff brush dipped in water. Pat abalone dry with paper towel. Scrub inside of shell well and set aside somewhere warm.

2 Using a small, sharp turning knife, carefully trim away tough frill – merely a few millimetres around outer edge of abalone. Lay abalone foot-side up and cut with a razor-sharp cook's knife into paper-thin slices.

3 Trim outer leaves from fennel and green garlic, then cut both as finely as possible and tip into a bowl with abalone and rub together with your hands. Make a coarse purée of basil and extra-virgin olive oil in a blender or mortar and pestle.

4 Shred lettuce leaves and make a nest on a serving plate, then put warm shell on top. Preheat a barbecue hotplate or a large frying pan until extremely hot, then drizzle with olive oil. Quickly scatter abalone, fennel and garlic as evenly as possible over entire surface and season swiftly. Toss immediately with a fish slice to sear for a mere second or two, then scrape with blinding efficiency into a wide, shallow bowl. Drizzle with basil oil and squeeze over lemon juice before gently tossing and serving in the shell.

Abalone served in the shell makes an ideal shared appetiser for two or an impressive centrepiece for a seafood antipasto.

oysters and Pearls

I get a mischievous kick out of serving oysters, knowing of their highly persuasive powers, yet have to confess to an embarrassing frigidity when it comes to swallowing one myself.

Exposure is everything, I guess. I remember as a child occasionally seeing oysters swimming in a jar in the fridge, but I can't recall seeing anyone actually eat one. But perhaps my single biggest hurdle in embracing this much-lauded mollusc is that I will never ever forget the stench from the oyster-bottling shop underneath my aunt and uncle's flat.

For the moment, I can proudly manage maybe two of the tiny Sydney rock species, although am still a tremulous virgin when it comes to an angassi, Pacific or bulging bluff. Without doubt, my seduction needs a little foreplay – for me, the whole ordeal relies heavily on salivating at the sight of those pristine juices, so I only imbibe when shucked on the spot!

In a quest to face my food phobia head on, my oyster appreciation took a turn for the better a few years back with the discovery of a little book sympathetically titled *Consider the Oyster*, by M.F.K. Fisher. I was thrilled to bits by the following distraction and have since looked at every oyster with new enthusiasm.

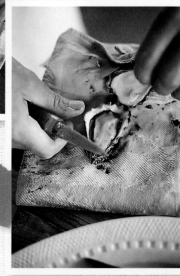

With a strong inbuilt oceanic pull, I have a romantic notion that one day I will be knife in hand, shucking oysters straight off the rocks!

To make a Pearl

1 healthy spat
1 mature oyster
1 bead
1 wire cage
ligatures
scrubbing brushes, etc.
unnameable wound-astringent provided by Japanese government
1 diving-girl

Introduce the spat, which should be at least $1/75$ of an inch long, to the smooth surface of the cage. Submerge him in quiet clean water, where the cage will protect him from starfish, and frequent inspections and scrubbings will keep his rapidly growing shell free from boring-worms and such pests.

In three years prepare him for the major operation of putting the bead on his mantle (epithelium). Once the bead is in place, draw the mantle over it and ligature the tissues to form a wee sac. Put the sac into a second oyster, remove the ligature, treat the wound with the unnameable astringent, and after the oyster has been caged, put him into the sea.

Supervise things closely for seven years, with the help of your diving-girl. Any time after that you may open your oyster, and you have about one chance in twenty of owning a marketable pearl, and a small but equally exciting chance of having cooked up something really valuable.

M. F. K. Fisher

71

Harbour Prawns or Blue-swimmer Crabs Deep-fried, with Aïoli

It is an exciting time in spring and summer when my fishmonger gets his hands on tiny green harbour prawns, literally from Botany Bay or other nooks around Sydney Harbour. Sometimes estuaries further up the coast, such as the Clarence River, flush out similarly sized school prawns, affectionately known as 'schoolies'. Both varieties are available sporadically at Sydney Fish Market at Pyrmont. (Of course, if you come across tiny green prawns at your fishmonger's, use these, whatever their name.)

Be sure to cook harbour prawns or schoolies the day you buy them, as they tend to oxidise in the head and turn an off-putting, darkening grey. The tiniest prawns are eaten whole, simply tossed in flour and swiftly fried, whereas the larger ones slide down a little more easily if their pointy beaks have been removed first with a snip from a sharp pair of kitchen scissors.

Unlike harbour prawns, blue-swimmer crabs (preferably from southern Australia) are best in the cooler months, as they spawn between November and January. Blue-swimmers graded 'extra large' from the cooler waters tend to be a consistent 350–400 g, whereas crabs of the same grading from the warmer waters off Queensland (not as sweet, I reckon) start at 500 g and can be as large as 1 kg! Select the plumpest, sweetest-smelling and most strikingly azure crab for this finger-licking treat, and ask your fishmonger to clean it for you. Cut the 'windows' in the shell, as described below, at home to make sure you expose a little extra meat to the flour and seasoning, the key to making the eating all the more fantastic. And use fine salt rather than flakes, as it doesn't fall off!

If cooking for a group, just multiply the following quantities accordingly, bearing in mind that the aïoli recipe yields enough for four. Please don't be tempted to cook more than one batch of prawns at a time as the oil will lose heat, and what should have been crispy treats will end up unappetisingly greasy.

SERVES 1

1 handful flat-leaf parsley

200 g green harbour or school prawns or 1 × 350–400 g blue-swimmer crab

1 litre sunflower or olive oil

½ cup plain flour

fine salt

freshly ground black pepper

Aïoli (see page 198)

lemon wedges

1 Wash parsley, then pick off leaves, discarding stems, and dry thoroughly. If your prawns aren't really tiny, pull their pointy beaks away.

2 Preheat oil to 200°C in a deep-fryer or a heavy-based pan large enough to hold double the volume (the oil will bubble up during cooking). When oil is hot, toss prawns with flour, coating well, then swiftly shake off excess and put into a frying basket or directly into oil. Fry for almost a minute until just lightly golden. Lift out frying basket (or remove prawns with a slotted spoon) and scatter with parsley. When oil has reheated, dunk prawns back in and fry for 3 seconds only (beware – the frying parsley will spit!). Drain prawns on paper towel and season well, then serve with aïoli, lemon wedges and perhaps a finger-bowl alongside.

3 If using crab, lay it on its back and squeeze in the middle where the belly flap meets the top shell. This will lift slightly, making it easier to peel back the top. Pull the dark, feathery gills away from each side and discard. Using a large knife, cut crab in half lengthways, then across into quarters, between the four legs. Pick out the 'mustard', if so inclined, then, using a sharp pair of kitchen scissors, cut top section of claw away nearest the joint and carefully snip and flick surface shell from flesh, exposing an access 'window' on each leg. Proceed as described for frying prawns, but initially fry for 1 minute longer until golden – check flesh is cooked in the middle by gently prising it apart.

Prawn Cutlets, Crumbed and Pan-fried, with Tartare Sauce

For the most sensational prawn cutlets, get hold of large, fresh (that is, green and not frozen) prawns, then crumb them with a light hand and make your own chunky tartare sauce.

SERVES **4–6**

12 large, fresh green prawns (about 1 kg)

⅓ cup oregano leaves

½ cup flat-leaf parsley leaves

¾ cup coarse breadcrumbs

1 egg

50 ml pouring cream

plain flour, for dusting

500 ml olive oil

salt

freshly ground black pepper

1 quantity Tartare Sauce (see page 197)

lemon wedges

1   Preheat oven to 100°C. Peel prawns, leaving on each tail end. Freeze heads for stock or for making Shellfish Oil (see page 195). Lay each prawn flat and run a small sharp knife down its 'back', then devein. Exaggerate this 'butterfly' cut by pressing firmly to splay prawn evenly.

2   Finely chop oregano and parsley and rub through breadcrumbs. Lightly whisk egg with cream in a bowl. Dust each prawn lightly with flour, shaking off excess before dipping into egg mixture, draining well and coating lightly in crumbs.

3   Heat half the olive oil in a frying pan large enough to take about half the prawns in a single layer, and line a baking tray with paper towel. Check oil is perfectly hot by gently dipping in tip of a prawn – the oil should bubble in response if hot enough. Ease each prawn in carefully, cut-side up to start with, and fry for about 1 minute a side until deep golden. Lift onto prepared tray with a slotted spoon and keep warm in oven. Quickly strain hot oil to remove any remnant crumbs, then return to pan with remaining oil and reheat. Fry second batch of prawns as above, then drain. Season prawn cutlets well before serving on a bed of tartare sauce with lemon wedges alongside.

Yabby Cocktail with Tomato Chutney Mayonnaise

I reckon the only improvement one can make to the classic shellfish cocktail is to insist on using the freshest shellfish available, be it crab, prawns, freshwater marron or yabbies. I like a few chunks of avocado in mine, and I use a dollop of homemade tomato chutney in the mayonnaise instead of pinking it up with tomato paste.

SERVES 4–6

12 extra-large live yabbies

salt

iced water

1 iceberg lettuce

1 small cucumber

6 spring onions

1 ripe avocado

extra-virgin olive oil

freshly ground black pepper

125 ml Mayonnaise (see page 196)

125 ml Tomato Chutney (see page 201)

1 lime or 2–3 finger limes

1 Sedate yabbies in a lidded container in freezer for about 30 minutes. Meanwhile, bring 5 litres water to a boil in a stockpot. Throw in 2 large handfuls cooking salt before carefully submerging yabbies, then cook for 5 minutes. Scoop out yabbies with a slotted spoon and chill in iced water until just cool enough to handle.

2 With one hand on the tail and the other on the head, twist each yabby head from body. Rinse off 'mustard' in head, if inclined (or add it to the mayonnaise), then snip down each side of tail with kitchen scissors to free meat from shell. Twist off claws where they connect to body, then use kitchen scissors to trim end straight. Using this end for access, carefully poke your scissors into left side of claw, snipping surface shell away from flesh about 1 cm up towards pincers. Repeat this on right-hand side. Carefully flick thin surface shell away to expose a 'window' of yabby meat, leaving pincers attached for handling. Repeat on underside, then cut tails in half lengthways and devein.

3 Core lettuce, then wash and shake or spin dry and shred thinly. Peel, seed and finely dice cucumber. Trim and finely slice spring onions. Cut avocado in half lengthways and scoop out flesh in one confident motion with a large spoon, then cut into dainty bite-sized chunks. Drizzle avocado with extra-virgin olive oil and season with salt and pepper.

4 Pile lettuce into a small serving bowl or goblet per person. Scatter with cucumber and spring onion, then add avocado. Glaze yabby tails with a little extra-virgin olive oil, then season and arrange on salad, slightly off-centre and showing their blushing side. Dollop with mayonnaise, then make a slight indentation with the back of your spoon and nestle in some tomato chutney. Sit claws alongside and serve with a wedge of lime.

Sardines Stuffed Sicilian-style

Every time I see plump fresh sardines I think back to those I had wrapped in Treviso radicchio leaves and grilled over coals in a seaside bar near Taormina in north-eastern Sicily. As a tribute to that memory, before wrapping sardines I like to fill each butterflied fish with a Sicilian-inspired stuffing featuring currants and pine nuts. Bound with sautéed onion, breadcrumbs, a few chopped olives, and some chilli, parsley and coriander, these deliciously sweet-and-sour sardines make an ideal starter, light lunch or antipasto.

You can butterfly the sardines yourself, of course, but you can also ask your fishmonger to do it for you.

SERVES **4–6**

12 fresh sardines (about 500 g)

1 onion

1 clove garlic

1 bird's-eye chilli

½ cup green olives

⅓ cup coriander leaves

⅓ cup flat-leaf parsley leaves

75 ml olive oil

⅓ cup pine nuts

1 cup coarse fresh breadcrumbs

⅓ cup currants

finely grated zest and juice of ½ lemon

salt

freshly ground black pepper

12 outer leaves from about 3 Treviso *or* large regular radicchio

25 ml good-quality red-wine *or* sherry vinegar

50 ml extra-virgin olive oil

1   To butterfly sardines, slit belly of each sardine and pull out and discard innards. Rinse under running water, then rub off scales. Cut off head and carefully pull out backbone, then flatten fillet. Pat butterflied sardines dry with paper towel and refrigerate while making stuffing.

2   Peel and finely dice onion. Peel garlic, then deseed chilli and mince both together. Pit olives and chop coarsely. Roughly chop coriander and parsley leaves.

3   Heat 50 ml olive oil in a large frying pan over a moderate flame, then add onion and pine nuts and cook for several minutes, stirring occasionally, until pale golden. Add garlic and chilli, then breadcrumbs, olives, currants, lemon zest and strained lemon juice. Stir well, then remove from heat and add chopped herbs. Season well to taste and leave to cool to room temperature.

4   Remove cores from radicchio leaves by cutting away a 3 cm V-shaped wedge. Lay a butterflied sardine on each leaf, then spoon filling onto one half of fish. Fold other half over stuffing, then wrap each fish snugly in its leaf.

5   Preheat a barbecue hotplate or large frying pan, then drizzle with remaining olive oil. Add wrapped sardines, pressing down with a fish slice, and cook for about 2 minutes a side. Serve drizzled with vinegar and extra-virgin olive oil and eat with your fingers, leaves and all!

Scallops Seared in the Half Shell, with Fennel Salsa

My favourite variety of scallop is the purple-blushed, thick-shelled 'queen' from Coffin Bay in South Australia or its rusty-bloomed sister from Tasmania's Spring Bay. Both come to market plump, with the roe left on, unlike the thinner, pale-shelled saucer scallops from Queensland that arrive with roe removed and suspiciously shaved flat, apparently with export in mind (these thin shells splinter and spit when I sear them, anyway, so good luck to 'em!).

At the time of writing my fishmonger told me of an exciting new seaweed farm under development in South Australia – how I'd love to use the real thing in this dish! In the meantime, a vibrant emerald bed of wilted 'frill-ice' lettuce does a beaut samphire impersonation here.

SERVES **4–6**
24 **Coffin Bay** *or* **Spring Bay scallops in the half shell**
olive oil
1 **frill-ice** *or* **other ruffled green lettuce**

FENNEL SALSA
1 **burstingly ripe tomato**
2 **cloves garlic**
1 **bird's-eye chilli**
1 **small red onion**
1 **large bulb fennel**
1 **handful flat-leaf parsley**
100 ml **extra-virgin olive oil**
finely grated zest and juice of 1 lemon
salt
freshly ground black pepper

1   Using a small turning knife, carefully remove half-moon, toenail-sized muscle opposite roe of each scallop in one smooth motion. Dip paper towel into cool water and wipe grit from around and under each scallop, checking with your fingers as you go, until clean. Dry scallop and shell with paper towel, then brush each scallop with olive oil and refrigerate while making salsa.

2   To make the fennel salsa, blanch, peel and cut tomato into 1 cm dice. Peel and mince garlic, then finely chop chilli (and deseed, if you wish). Peel and finely dice onion. Finely dice fennel, saving a few feathery tips to chop coarsely with parsley. Combine salsa vegetables and herbs with extra-virgin olive oil, lemon zest and strained juice and season well.

3   Core lettuce, then wash and shake or spin dry and separate leaves (you'll need several per plate). Heat a barbecue hotplate or very large, heavy-based frying pan, then drizzle with olive oil. Sear lettuce leaves a few at a time for several seconds, then turn swiftly for a second on the other side and remove. Spread leaves on a serving platter or individual plates.

4   Remove scallops from fridge. Sear in their shells flesh-side down for a few seconds until appetisingly golden brown, then turn swiftly. Immediately spoon a teaspoonful of salsa inside each shell opposite roe. A few seconds later the scallops will be just cooked – look at them side-on to check for a whitening translucency. Serve scallops in their half shells at once on their bed of lettuce.

Tasmanian Ocean Trout Steeped Whole in Tarragon

On a fishing trip north of Broome, with frozen prawns from the bait'n'tackle shop, we landed a not-so-handsome coral cod that, we found, 'stood' rather neatly curled inside our pot. We covered it with sea water, threw in a twist of lemongrass and simmered it over a low flame until it was just about to boil, then off the heat it came. Our sea stock became a rather murky affair, but the heady scent of lemongrass kept us enthused. We lifted our cod (now all the uglier with bulging white eyes) out of his pond and onto a plate before sliding off his leathery cloak. Our beast was now gleaming with a whole new inner beauty, and we all agreed his pearly white meat surpassed the finest lobster. Back in the city, this simmering fish got me thinking, although I'm reluctant to insult any fish by steeping it in the waters of Bondi!

With a lazy summer's lunch in mind, this ocean trout is extremely easy, stress-free (prepared a day ahead) and makes an impressive central dish, served whole as though it has just swum onto the plate. Once the fish skin has been slipped away, the moist flesh glistens all the more, glazed with a dressing of chopped tarragon and its own sparkling roe. Mignonette lettuce hearts make a dainty accompaniment, and a potato salad dressed with tartare sauce is all that's needed. Everyone will love the theatre of this dish!

If you have a suitably sized piece of muslin to hand you can parcel up all the vegetables that accompany the poaching fish, tying it tightly at each end to make a large sausage. This can then be placed underneath the fish, a help when you come to lift out the fish, and will also save you from having to brush the vegetables from the fish afterwards. Handy, but not essential.

SERVES **8**

1 × 2 kg Tasmanian ocean trout

1 large carrot

1 large onion

1 stick celery

8 tablespoons salt

2 tablespoons castor sugar

4 cloves garlic

2 generous handfuls French tarragon

1 orange

1 lemon

100 ml extra-virgin olive oil

150–200 g ocean trout roe

freshly ground black pepper

salt flakes

16 mignonette lettuce

1 Lower trout into a suitably large pot so it can 'swim' upright, comfortably curled along the sides of the pot – my pot is 25 cm wide and 16 cm deep. Coarsely grate carrot, onion and celery and add to pot with salt and castor sugar. Peel and crush 3 of the cloves of garlic, then add to pot with half the tarragon. Fill pot with enough cold water to just cover fish (3.5 litres in mine) and stand over a moderate flame. Bring to a simmer verging on a boil (95°C, if testing with a thermometer), then turn off flame swiftly. Leave to cool to room temperature for several hours, then refrigerate overnight, still submerged.

2 To serve the next day, zest and juice orange and lemon, then make a dressing by whisking juices and zest with finely chopped remaining garlic clove, remaining picked and chopped tarragon leaves and extra-virgin olive oil. Stir in trout roe, then season well to taste and pour into a serving jug. Remove outer leaves from lettuce to reveal hearts only (keep outer leaves for another use), then, keeping hearts whole, wash and shake or spin dry.

3 When you are ready to eat, carefully lift fish from poaching stock with a fish slice in each hand, then drain for several minutes on paper towel. Meanwhile, seat your guests and ready them for the spectacle. Stand trout on a serving platter as if it was swimming along plate and arrange mignonette hearts around fish, then carry the platter to the table with aplomb. Using a small, sharp knife, make an incision on either side of the backbone and gently peel away skin and discard. Pour dressing generously over fish and lettuce. Serve with a potato salad dressed with Tartare Sauce (see page 197).

Tommy Ruff, Butterflied, Filled with Olives, Wrapped in Pancetta and Pan-fried

Allow me to introduce Tommy Ruff, a much-neglected saltwater herring endemic to the cooler waters of southern Australia and, perhaps due to his puny size, often snubbed as bait. Bursting with healthy omega oils and somewhat dark of flesh, he is happiest among the company of those robust Mediterraneans – olives, garlic, basil and pancetta. Any fishmonger worth his salt will do the scaling, gutting and butterflying for you, so I hope you will befriend my mate Tommy Ruff too!

SERVES 4–6

150 g large green olives
2 cloves garlic
finely grated zest and juice of 1 large lemon
24 paper-thin slices flat pancetta
24 large basil leaves
12 butterflied Tommy Ruffs
200 ml extra-virgin olive oil
salt
freshly ground black pepper
1 pinch castor sugar
olive oil

1 Pit olives by arranging flat inside a plastic bag and bashing appropriately with a meat mallet. After removing pips, chop olives coarsely with peeled garlic cloves. Stir lemon zest through olive mixture.

2 Arrange half the pancetta slices on a clean workbench with plenty of space in between. Put a basil leaf about a quarter of the way down each slice, crossways, with greener side facing down. Lay upper half of a butterflied fillet skin-side down, so that leaf falls underneath left-hand side, then spread left-hand half of fillet evenly with olive mixture and fold other side over filling. In reverse, lay a basil leaf on pancetta as previously, then carefully begin to wrap pancetta around each fillet, 'winding' it down the fish as you go and introducing a second slice when the first finishes. The aim is to encase the fish in pancetta, with a basil leaf neatly caught on either side.

3 Make a dressing by whisking extra-virgin olive oil with strained lemon juice and seasoning with salt, pepper and a little castor sugar for balance.

4 Heat a barbecue hot plate or large frying pan for several minutes before drizzling with a little olive oil, then carefully lower each fish onto hot plate or pan. Turn fish after about 2 minutes to crisp other side. Gently insert a small knife to check if fish is cooked – the flesh should be just opaque. Serve drizzled with dressing.

A few thin slices of blanched fennel make the ideal bed for 'Tommies' and all their juices.

Mud Crab

In the 1970s, my Dad and his mates threw annual day-long 'chilli mudcrab' parties that were a thrill beyond all hedonistic imaginings – a chilli challenge so fired with enthusiasm my tongue and lips would throb all night.

On a camping trip north of Broome a few years back I was lucky enough to share a catch with Linda, a local Bardi woman. Out of frugal respect for the catch, Linda would sit the freshly pulled crab backs on the fire so the innards could slowly stew inside the shell, the flavour so intense it punished any days of decadent wastefulness.

These days I love to steam/stew mud crab with a little wine, the precious juices thickened with ground rice. To the puritan, perhaps, the addition of corn and leeks is superfluous, although their natural sweetness nicely rounds off the saltiness of the crab.

Whether you acquire your live crab from a fishmarket or by spending a day in the mangroves (with local guide) poking around with a stick, cook your crab as soon as you can! After a day the crab will resort to 'eating' itself – an ingenious internal leaching that will leave the flesh mushy, and you really disappointed.

And, of course, add as much chilli as you like.

SERVES 2

2 × 1 kg live mud crabs
1 cob corn
1 leek
2 cloves garlic
2 tablespoons rice
100 ml olive oil
350 ml dry white wine
1 teaspoon castor sugar
freshly ground black pepper

1 Sedate crabs in freezer for about 30 minutes. Lay each crab on its back and, using a large cleaver, chop deeply into its underbelly between the eyes, trying not to damage carapace – this kills the crab but keeps the large top shell whole for later use. (I find it best to do this halfway first, completing the cut after spinning the crab and aligning a second strike.)

2 Holding crab firmly over a fine-meshed strainer sitting in a small bowl to catch juices, push belly flap, which will lift carapace a little, making it easier to remove. Scrape innards inside shell into strainer and scrub off all fine, clinging mud, then rinse shell thoroughly and set aside. Trying to catch all juices as you go, strip away grey gills and 'mustard' between, wiping away all mud with a damp cloth (as opposed to rinsing). Using cleaver again, cut crab in half lengthways, then across into quarters between the four legs. Swiftly crack each main claw with flat of cleaver. Discard contents of strainer, reserving juices and prepared crab.

3 Strip ears and silk from corn and cut kernels away from cob by running a sharp cook's knife down sides. Avoid cutting into husk and applying too much pressure (you'll get mush!). Discard outer layer from leek, then trim roots and slice lengthways, then across into about 2 mm wide pieces. Wash well by dunking into water in a strainer, then drain. Peel and roughly chop garlic. Pound rice to a coarse powder in a mortar and pestle.

4 Heat olive oil in a heavy-based, medium-sized pan over a moderate flame. Sauté garlic for several seconds until light golden. Add leek and corn and sweat for several minutes, stirring regularly with a wooden spoon to avoid any browning or catching. Pour in wine, ground rice, crab pieces and saved juices and stir swiftly. Top with reserved carapace, then cover with a lid. Cook for a total of 5 minutes, removing shell once nicely blushed and rolling crab in sauce and stirring as needed. Season with sugar and add pepper to taste – I find there is usually no need to add any salt.

5 Serve crab with sauce spooned over and topped with its shell, and have the appropriate picks, crackers, finger-bowls and napkins on hand.

Live mud crabs make for →
memorable meals. Whenever
I've had the chance to eat a
mudcrab, like most, I devour
every ounce of flesh, suck every
joint clean, until nothing is left.

Jewfish Cutlets Braised with Preserved Lemon, Basil and Peas

Often confused with West Australian dhufish (also known as pearl perch), the slightly underrated jew can be caught all over the coastline. I love the full-flavoured, soft, unctuous flesh of jewfish braised as a cutlet, and the commingling of lemon with peas and basil in this dish. Serve with crisp fried potatoes to mop up the juices.

SERVES 6

1 × 4 kg whole jewfish or 6 × 300–350 g cutlets

4 handfuls spinach leaves

2 cloves garlic

200 ml extra-virgin olive oil

1 generous handful basil leaves

1 piece preserved lemon (equivalent to ¼ lemon)

200 g peas in the pod

⅓ teaspoon cumin seeds

125 ml white wine

250 ml Fish Stock (see page 192)

juice of 1 lemon

salt

freshly ground black pepper

olive oil

1   If using a whole fish, ensure all scales are removed. Using a sharp pair of kitchen scissors, snip away dorsal fins running along top of fish. With a large, sharp cook's knife, cut 6 × 2 cm thick cutlets from central (most evenly thick) part of the fish. When your knife hits the backbone, rock knife slightly from left to right to find a joint between vertebrae and continue cutting through. Fillet remaining flesh from tail end and save for Fish Stew for Two (see page 96) and save head and tailbone for making a fish stock.

2   Remove stalks from spinach, then wash and shake or spin dry. Peel and mince garlic. Using a mortar and pestle, make a coarse purée with half the garlic, half the extra-virgin olive oil and the basil leaves. Remove excess flesh and pith from preserved lemon and cut rind into small dice. Pod peas. In a small dry frying pan, toast cumin seeds over a low flame until fragrant, then cool and grind.

3   Ten minutes before serving, preheat oven to 220°C. Heat remaining extra-virgin olive oil over a full flame in a suitably large, heavy-based, preferably non-stick frying pan. Pat cutlets dry with paper towel. Carefully lower each cutlet into hot oil 'away from you' to avoid spitting. Cook cutlets for several minutes until deep golden, then carefully turn and cook for several seconds longer. Drain all excess oil from pan, leaving cutlets in place, before deglazing it with wine, stock and lemon juice, then scatter with diced preserved lemon and season well. Slide pan into hot oven for 7 minutes until fish nearest to bone is just cooked.

4   Meanwhile, warm serving plates and a platter. Bring a small saucepan of salted water to a boil and add peas. Heat a drizzle of olive oil in a wide stainless-steel saucepan, then add remaining garlic and sauté for several seconds until nut brown. Add ground cumin and stir in spinach leaves swiftly until wilted, then season well before draining and arranging loosely on warmed plates.

5   Using a fish slice, carefully lift cutlets onto a warm platter. Stand frying pan over a full flame and reduce cooking liquor for several minutes to a saucing consistency. Lay cutlets on spinach beds. Tip any juices on platter into sauce with basil oil and combine with a swirl. Check peas are tender, then drain and add to sauce before spooning over each cutlet.

Catch of the Day

There's talk of a trip in the dinghy,
big prospect of fish to bake.
So what have ya got for burley?
And what do ya use for bait?

Pop Hill was as protective of his old pillowcase as Nanna Hill was about filling it. The closest I got to the burley was when I'd peer into the water to watch it float around from the back of the boat like confetti, slowly sinking and vanishing among frenzied flashes of silver. I remember the smell of garlic and what looked like cracked wheat, then Pop would roll up little balls of his 'magic' bait (we wouldn't dare hook our own) and we'd be off. Fish tugged within minutes and, despite a chaotic tangle of lines, we always managed to land enough bream – filleted, floured and pan-fried – to feed the eight or so of our extended family.

Years on, up in the Daintree, I'm a bit more ambitious. The pro we're with is angling for barra. He cuts the engine to drift for a bit, then leaps to the front of the boat. With a swirl through the air with the net, he lassoes the surface of the water before dragging the net back. Now we're set with our sparkle of bait . . .

It takes a while to get the gist of it all as our lines drag through the water with heavy pulls and cunning darts towards the mangroves before it's on for young and old. One by one the gang starts to reel in all types of colourful estuary cod, grunter and queenies, when I trump them with the elusive mangrove Jack, a highly prized table fish with a handsome rust blush – the envy of all on board. With dinner in mind we start to share stories and serving suggestions. Our guide talks of lying the catch in hot coals, each fish rolled in tea-tree bark or wrapped in clay.

Which brings me to the salt crust... Back at our base the fire is lit as I rummage through the cupboards for flour and salt. I empty both packets onto the bench, save some flour for rolling – I have twice as much flour as salt. With just enough water to bind, I start to scrape and squeeze the dough together. A slight dusting of flour is all that's needed to stop the dough sticking to the bench, and a bottle does for a rolling pin. Soon the dough is about 2 mm thick, which will do the trick for at least three of our fish. Each is gift-wrapped, with the dough pinched lovingly together along the sides. The flames have died down to expose a mere glow of coals, so I bury in our parcels. I reckon they need just under 20 minutes, which gives me just enough time to boil up some spuds and make a salad.

A comforting smell of damper fills the air as the dough begins to darken. We unearth our parcels, dust 'em off and peel away the blackened tops, then slide the skin from each fish to reveal the flesh, glistening in its own juices. Each fish somehow manages to have sucked the perfect amount of salt from its crust, and all are sublime. Surely the most memorable fish to eat is the one you've caught yourself!

Barramundi Braised with Ratatouille

I find it encouraging that the question I'm often asked when serving barramundi over any other fish is whether it's farmed or wild. Perhaps this is asked with subtle concern for the dwindling supply of fish in the sea, or maybe there's a real awareness of the difference in flavour between the two. Some are partial to the muddier-tasting wild catch, while others are adamant that a farmed fish is cleaner on the palate.

I must admit to feeling slightly torn about the issue of fish farming. For years I insisted on buying only wild barramundi to serve in the restaurant. Sometimes the flavour overwhelmed and sometimes the adrenalin released by the fish when being trawled through the water (as opposed to being line-caught and spiked) would cause the flesh to toughen, and we can't blame the fish for that.

As a restaurateur, with consistency a major consideration, the exciting endeavours of aquaculture have provided a comforting safety net. At appropriate times, we can still acquire our national fish, wild, as our Department of Fisheries monitors its sustainability. I encourage you to enquire if your fish is wild or farmed, so that you too can learn and enjoy the many characteristics of both.

This recipe is designed for individually portioned, skin-on fillets. Ask your fishmonger to scale and fillet an appropriately sized whole fish and grab the bones for stock. The silk aubergine here is my favourite cream-and-purple variety, and the flowering zucchini can be ordered from a good greengrocer or purloined from an accommodating friend's vegie patch, if you don't have one of your own!

SERVES 4

1 aubergine

salt

1 burstingly ripe tomato

1 tablespoon balsamic vinegar

2 cloves garlic

1 red pepper

8 small flowering zucchini (courgettes)

1 small red onion

olive oil

4 × 250 g barramundi fillets
  (skin on and about 1 cm thick)

125 ml dry white wine or Fish Stock (see page 192)

1 tablespoon extra-virgin olive oil

freshly ground black pepper

6 basil leaves

1   Using a vegetable peeler or small, sharp knife and working from top to bottom, cut away 1 cm wide strips of aubergine skin to leave a zebra-striped pattern of flesh and skin. Cut aubergine into 1 cm chunks, then sprinkle with fine salt and leave to sweat for about 30 minutes. Meanwhile, blanch, peel and cut tomato into 1 cm chunks, then drizzle with vinegar and set aside. Peel and crush garlic and put on top of tomato. Halve pepper and remove seeds, then peel with a vegetable peeler before cutting into 1 cm chunks. Wipe zucchini free of any grit and trim off ends. Peel onion and cut into chunks.

2   Preheat oven to 200°C. Dry aubergine with paper towel. Pour olive oil into a large ovenproof frying pan to a depth of 5 mm and heat over a moderate flame. When hot, fry aubergine until deep golden, tossing, then drain on paper towel. Leave just enough oil in pan to cover base with a thin film.

3   Dab skin-side of each fillet with paper towel and lay in pan, skin-side down, when oil has reheated. Press down firmly on each fillet for a few moments to help skin crisp evenly. Using a fish slice, lift each fillet carefully and check skin for hot spots (indicated by scorching – in this case, lower heat and move fish), then continue pan-frying until skin is evenly coloured and crisp. Add flowering zucchini to pan and scatter in onion. After a few moments, turn zucchini and fish, then add wine or stock and extra-virgin olive oil and season well. Slide pan into hot oven for 6–7 minutes until fish is just cooked – check by carefully lifting skin. Meanwhile, warm plates and a platter.

4   Lift fish onto warmed platter, then add tomato mixture to pan with fried aubergine and boil for a few seconds, swirling pan to help amalgamate sauce. Sprinkle in torn basil leaves, then spoon onto plates and serve at once, topped with barra.

Skate Wings Pan-fried with Black Butter and Capers

Skate has a short, slender, thorny tail, unlike his relation the stingray. Skate and ray flesh has a unique texture, much like a piano-accordion of tender, tiny chicken fillets, and is hard to beat pan-fried in the classic French bistro manner, with black butter and capers. The butter is traditionally bound by an acid springboard of vinegar, although I prefer the fresh flavour of lemon and the Mediterranean lift from a little garlic. As large skate requires an initial poaching for even cooking (and easier removal of skin and central cartilage), ask your fishmonger to skin and fillet smaller, plate-sized fish about 2 cm thick.

SERVES 2

1 generous handful flat-leaf parsley

1 clove garlic

finely grated zest and juice of 1 large lemon

1 generous handful capers (preferably large ones in brine)

2 × 250g skate wing halves (about 1 cm thick)

plain flour, for dusting

150 g butter

salt

freshly ground black pepper

1 Wash parsley and shake or spin dry before coarsely chopping with peeled garlic, then mixing through lemon zest. If using capers in brine, squeeze well; wash salted capers thoroughly, rubbing well to free them of excess salt, then dry with paper towel.

2 Dust skate lightly with flour. Melt butter in your largest frying pan over a full flame until a deep caramel. Carefully lower in skate 'away from you' to avoid spitting, then season well. Cook for several moments until nicely browned, then gently turn with a fish slice. Scatter capers into gaps around skate to fry, then season well again. After several moments check skate is cooked by testing to see if flesh segments separate easily, then gently swerve pan to fry capers evenly and aid even blackening of butter. Once skate is cooked, add parsley mixture and fry for a split second. Pour in strained lemon juice (beware of violent spitting), then remove pan from heat and swirl to combine butter and herbs.

3 Serve skate immediately on warmed plates with sauce spooned over and accompanied by boiled potatoes and perhaps steamed greens or a salad on the side.

Once halved, an ergonomically round skate wing is ideal for two and should fit comfortably into your largest frying pan.

Fish Stew for Two

Naturally the success of any fish stew, be it a French bouillabaisse, an Italian Livornese or my version below, relies on the freshness of the fish. Gutsy, well-balanced flavour extraction from a stock-based 'essence' is also paramount, with the final stewing moments precisely nurtured so that each morsel is cooked to perfection.

The essence for this recipe has a bisque-like strength, having been made on a fish stock base, simmered for an hour, then crushed through a Mouli and finished in an Italian manner with olive oil for gloss (and health) instead of cream.

I'm particularly fond of this combination of fish, but of course anything can be substituted to suit personal taste and availability. For best results (and perhaps because the size of the pan required is a limiting factor), I strongly suggest keeping this dish intimate.

1 × 250 g scaled, skin-on fillet of thick-fleshed fish (such as barramundi, jewfish or Bass groper)
4 plump scallops in the shell (such as Coffin Bay or Spring Bay, preferably roe on)
12 mussels
2 large bugs *or* 4 green prawns
2 kipfler potatoes
1 handful shallots
2 cloves garlic
1 handful cavolo nero *or* spinach leaves
1 bird's-eye chilli (optional)
150 ml extra-virgin olive oil
150 ml dry white wine
500 ml Fish Essence (see page 194)
1 handful freshly shelled *or* frozen peas
salt
freshly ground black pepper

1   Cut fish lengthways into 4 even pieces 1–1.5 cm thick. Using a small turning knife, carefully remove half-moon, toenail-sized muscle opposite roe of each scallop in one smooth motion. Dip paper towel into cool water and wipe grit from around and under each scallop, checking with your fingers as you go, until clean. Scrub dirt from mussels and twist off furry beards with a sharp, downwards tug. If using bugs, cut each in half from head to tail using a sharp cook's knife, then remove guts and discard. Alternatively, peel and devein prawns, leaving tail end attached and saving shells for stock.

2   Bring potatoes to a boil in cold water and cook until just tender, then drain. When cool enough to handle, rub off skins and cut into rounds. Peel and thinly slice shallots. Peel and mince garlic. Strip cavolo nero or spinach leaves from stalks, then wash well and shake or spin dry. If using chilli, cut in half, then deseed and mince flesh.

3   Ten minutes before serving, heat a deep, wide frying pan with half the extra-virgin olive oil over a moderate flame. Sauté shallots for about a minute until limp, then add garlic and sauté until slightly golden. Deglaze pan with wine and fish essence. Swiftly arrange cavolo nero leaves, fish (skin-side up) and all shellfish snugly in pan. Swirl around liquid, then add peas and chilli, if using, and tuck in potato slices. Cover with a lid and stew over a moderate flame for several minutes, gently shaking pan every 30 seconds or so, checking fish, scallops and bugs until just cooked and mussels have opened.

4   Lift fish and shellfish out into wide, warmed bowls, then add remaining extra-virgin olive oil to pan, reduce heat slightly and cook briefly to combine. Taste and adjust seasoning as required before pouring sauce over fish and serving with plenty of good bread alongside for mopping up the precious juices.

Duck Liver Pâté with Pulled Bread and Sweet-and-sour Onions

This pâté is pretty much a staple in the restaurant and, if it's not 'chalked up', we try to keep the wherewithal on hand to help sedate the regulars.

Choose plump, full-flavoured livers from ducks that are free-range and/or corn-fed. The Italian-style sweet-and-sour ('agro-dolce') onions bounce perfectly off the creamed livers, and the hedgehog pieces of 'pulled' bread give great textural crunch.

According to Elizabeth David's *English Bread and Yeast Cookery*, bread 'pulling' originated in England, where doughy centres of undercooked loaves were torn out for rebaking – a peasant frugality served plain or rubbed in dripping. In the restaurant we make 'pillows' of our malt bread specifically for 'pulling' but bake them all the way through (the hollowed shells make a great staff meal filled with tuna, tomato, onion, chick peas and garlic, all baked with a few herbs). Any good unsliced loaf will do, though. And rather than dripping, we drizzle our best extra-virgin over the hot, crusty pieces.

SERVES 4–6
2 large onions
2 cloves garlic
1 × 1 cm thick piece flat pancetta
125 ml Duck or Chook Stock (see page 191)
1 small handful oregano leaves
500 g free-range duck livers
100 ml olive oil
salt
freshly ground black pepper
50 ml balsamic vinegar
200 g butter
1 loaf malt bread (see page 10) *or* other good-quality bread
extra-virgin olive oil

SWEET-AND-SOUR ONIONS
3 large red onions
50 ml olive oil
1 tablespoon castor sugar
125 ml red wine
125 ml balsamic vinegar
⅓ cup currants
1 tablespoon lemon thyme leaves
salt
freshly ground black pepper

1   To make the sweet-and-sour onions, peel, quarter and slice onions. Heat olive oil in a large, shallow frying pan, then add onion and castor sugar and caramelise over a moderate flame. Deglaze pan with wine and vinegar. Add currants and continue to reduce over heat until liquid coats the back of a spoon. Add thyme leaves and season well. Remove from heat and allow to cool to room temperature.

2   Peel and roughly dice onions, then peel and roughly chop garlic. Cut pancetta into rough chunks and sauté with onion and garlic in a frying pan over moderate heat until caramelised. Deglaze pan with stock and add oregano. Meanwhile, trim livers of connective tissue, cutting away any green-stained (and bile-tasting) liver. Heat olive oil in a heavy-based frying pan and sauté livers until just firm but pink on the inside. Season well. Deglaze pan with vinegar. Pass livers and pancetta and onion mixture through a Mouli or sieve with butter, then purée in a blender until smooth. Check seasoning. Allow to set in desired mould.

3 Twenty minutes before serving, preheat oven to 200°C. Pull generous chunks of bread from centre of cut loaf and put onto a baking tray. Rebake pulled bread in hot oven for about 10 minutes until golden and crisped around edges. Serve duck liver pâté with warm pulled bread drizzled generously with your best extra-virgin olive oil and sweet-and-sour onions alongside.

Duck Legs, Preserved, with Potato Cakes, Figs and Spinach

Considering the classic French technique of preserving duck, known as *confit de canard*, has the most frugal of origins, it really need not intimidate the home cook.

First, find yourself a free-range duck weighing about 2 kg, with neck intact, and preferably with liver and gizzards. Traditionally, the process begins with separating the legs from the carcass, however the technique I use keeps both legs and breasts attached to the bone, maximising flavour and avoiding any ugly protrusion of the thigh bones as the meat cooks. Sit the duck on its back and dry with a paper towel, if necessary. Pull globs of excess fat from inside the cavity and place in a small saucepan with 2 tablespoons of water for rendering (see below). Using a large knife, cut a 'V' adjacent to the wishbone where the breasts meet the neck, then cut off neck. Pull neck skin free from its bone by turning inside out; save bone for stock. If not making Duck-neck Sausage (see page 105), add skin to rendering pan. Next, use your fingers to determine where breast meat ends, just inside each leg, then insert knife and cut persuasively down to the backbone, cutting the bird in half. Either roast the breasts on the bone or use to make duck-neck sausage.

The duck legs are then simmered in the duck's own rendered fat. To render or melt the fat, simply place the pan over a low heat for about an hour until the skin is golden and crisp, then strain and leave to cool to room temperature before transferring the fat to a sterilised jar and placing in the refrigerator, where it will keep for several months. An average duck will yield about 400 g of fat, so unless you already have a supply of duck fat on hand, your first batch of preserved duck will need to be topped up with another 400 g or so of duck or goose fat (available at most good delicatessens).

In anyone's language, preserved duck, if meltingly tender, well-crisped and nestled on a bed of sautéed leaves with a few perfectly ripe figs is surely the ultimate supper!

SERVES 2

350 g potatoes (sebago work well here)
salt
1 generous handful spinach leaves
1 clove garlic
200 ml reduced Duck Stock (see page 191)
1 teaspoon red-wine or sherry vinegar
freshly ground black pepper
castor sugar (optional)
4 ripe figs

PRESERVED DUCK LEGS

2 duck legs, prepared as outlined in recipe introduction
3 cloves garlic
1 handful thyme
1 heaped tablespoon juniper berries
1 heaped tablespoon coarse salt
800 g rendered duck fat

1 For preserved duck legs, firmly press on duck legs to flatten then place in ceramic or glass dish. Peel and lightly crush garlic and rub over legs, along with thyme. Using a pestle and mortar or spice grinder, grind juniper berries with salt then sprinkle evenly all over duck legs. Cover and refrigerate overnight.

2 The next day, pat duck legs dry with paper towel. Put duck fat into a deep, heavy-based pan and place over a low heat for several minutes until melted and warm. Carefully lower in duck legs and leave to simmer gently (at 90°C, if using a thermometer) for at least 1 hour or until meat is tender when tested with a skewer in thickest part of leg. Remove pan from heat, then carefully lift legs from fat by supporting each one underneath with a sturdy fish slice to avoid damaging the skin. Leave at room temperature to cool.

3 Remove legs from backbone by cutting skin halfway around thickest part of leg then gently lifting out meat; check underside of legs from any surface bone still attached. Place duck legs in a suitably wide, preferably ceramic, ovenproof dish, then pour fat through a fine sieve to completely cover them, leaving behind any juices lurking at the bottom of the pan (these could harbour unwelcome bacteria that might ruin the preserved duck legs). Leave at least overnight before using. Preserved duck legs will keep for at least a month is properly immersed in fat and refrigerated – just be gentle when you delve into the solid fat so as not to damage the skin of the duck.

4 Peel and quarter potatoes, then bring to a boil over a full flame in a small saucepan of cold water with a large pinch of salt. Once boiling, swiftly pour into a colander and leave to cool to room temperature. Coarsely grate cooled potato and form into 4 cakes about 6 cm round and 1 cm thick by pressing firmly. For greater crunch, a slight fraying around the edge is preferred. Pick leaves from spinach, then wash and spin or shake dry. Peel and finely mince garlic.

5 Preheat oven to 180°C. Put duck legs and their fat into oven in a heavy-based baking dish for about 10 minutes until fat has melted completely and duck has just warmed through, then remove. Carefully lift legs into a suitably large frying pan, skin-side down, and keep warm. Strain and reserve duck fat.

6 Pour duck fat into a frying pan to a depth of 5 mm and heat over a moderate flame. When hot, gently lower in potato cakes and shallow-fry for several minutes on each side until deep golden, then drain on paper towel and keep warm.

7 Reduce stock with vinegar for several minutes to a saucing consistency, then check seasoning (a sprinkling of castor sugar may help to balance acidity). Meanwhile, heat a drizzle of duck fat in frying pan, then sauté garlic for a second or two until just nut-brown before adding spinach leaves. Season, then sauté for a moment, shaking pan and tossing constantly with tongs. Tip spinach into a fine-meshed strainer to drain before arranging loosely on warmed plates. Meanwhile, crisp duck skin in frying pan over a moderate flame until evenly caramelised. Tear or cut figs in half and warm in sauce before serving – sit the legs alongside the spinach on some of the figgy sauce to retain their crispness.

A slice or two of this textural sausage
makes a lovely entrée or light lunch,
accompanied by a few salad leaves
drizzled with the roasting juices.

Duck-neck Sausage

I love using every possible part of a duck. Making a solitary sausage might seem fussy, but once you preserve the legs, start using the rendered fat, or crack braising the legs as described over the page, you'll be over the moon about how frugal and clever you've been! A couple of slices of duck-neck sausage work well with a braised leg.

MAKES **1**

1 small onion

1 × 2 mm thick slice flat pancetta

1 handful sage leaves

1 clove garlic

1 tablespoon duck fat

1 tablespoon pine nuts

1 tablespoon raisins

2 tablespoons coarse fresh breadcrumbs

finely grated zest of 1 orange

2 duck breasts

salt

freshly ground black pepper

1 duck liver (optional)

1 duck neck (skin only)

1   Peel and finely dice onion. Finely dice pancetta. Coarsely chop sage leaves and peel and mince garlic. Melt duck fat in a small frying pan over a moderate flame until hot. Add pancetta, onion and pine nuts and sauté for several minutes, stirring regularly, until nicely caramelised. Add garlic and sage leaves, then sauté for several seconds before adding raisins, breadcrumbs and orange zest. Remove from heat.

2   Trim away all excess skin protruding from edge of breast meat, remove all silver sinew, then cut meat into 5 mm dice. Add duck meat to onion mixture, then season generously. Trim liver, if using, of connective tissue, then double-check for and cut away any green-stained (and bile-tasting) liver. Tie narrowest end of neck skin tightly with butcher's twine. Stuff neck with mixture and insert both halves of liver at suitable intervals so they sit snugly towards middle of sausage, then tie with twine to seal larger end (depending on the length of the neck and whether you include the liver, you may have a little stuffing left over).

3   Preheat oven to 180°C. Heat a small ovenproof frying pan over a moderate flame. Add sausage, then season and sauté for several minutes, turning regularly, until lightly coloured on all sides. Transfer pan to oven for 30 minutes, turning sausage every 10 minutes until cooked. Remove from oven and put sausage onto a warm plate to rest somewhere warm for around 20 minutes. Slice to serve – with sautéed red cabbage and perhaps a few slices of beetroot baked until tender in foil, then reheated in the sauce from braised duck legs (see overleaf).

Take One Duck

I'm at the shack, I've stoked the Aga and I have the whole day to play. I have a duck to deal with.

One CHOP with my cleaver and it's off with the neck, then I strip back the skin while holding on tight to the bone inside. The fatty skin goes into a smallish pot with just a splash of water, then I slide the pot to the simmer side of the stove. The neck bone lands in its own hungry braising pan. Next, I cut each breast from the carcass, peeling away the tiny fillets underneath (sneaky treats for a food-obsessed dog), then set them aside, plotting a prosciutto-like cure later on. I hack free the ribcage (into the braising pan it goes) and leave the legs attached to their bone. With the force of both hands, I squash the legs to snap them flat – splayed like a cane toad up north on the road. Like a vulture I tear off any leftover globs to top up my rendering pot.

With my fat melting away nicely, I grab a few vegies to braise with the legs for lunch. I peel and roughly slice a large onion and scatter it in with the bones. One carrot will do, so I coarsely grate it in. A stick of celery gets stripped of its leaves before it's sliced and added with a few smashed cloves of garlic and juniper berries. I chuck in a bay leaf and a large sprig of thyme, then drizzle the lot with a spoonful from the rendering pot and sit the braising pan over a full flame.

In no time the pan starts to sizzle. After a minute or two, I poke away with my wooden spoon, rolling and pushing the bones and vegies to stop them getting too dark. Another minute or two passes and all's nicely golden brown, so I pour in half a bottle of red wine and the same amount of water. I sit my duck legs neatly on top with a generous seasoning of salt and a few twists of the pepper mill, then slide the pan into the moderate oven, the rest of our lunch now in mind.

I grab two large spuds; give them a quick scrub and then sit them in the oven on the shelf underneath the duck. I head to my patch in the garden, remembering the rainbow chard dancing merrily up the back.

Almost an hour has passed and a sweetly spiced aroma's drawing me back to the stove. I can't help but swirl the pan around and baste the legs with their bubbling stock. The spuds aren't far off, too, so it's time to wash that colourful chard, strip off the leaves and roughly slice the stalks.

The waft from the duck's getting too much to bear and I'm thrilled when I open the door – the skin's all golden and crisp, the sauce deeply glossed and everything perfectly caramelised around the edges. I sit the pan on the other hotplate, lift out the legs to my board to rest and gently spoon the film of fat directly into a waiting wide frying pan. In a moment or two I scatter in the chard stalks to sauté, with a toss of a spoon now and then. The pan gets another shake, then I lay in the leaves with a splash of water and a scatter of salt and pepper as the sauce spits for my attention. A slurp of water settles it down, then I finally get to dip in my spoon. WOW! It's gutsy and unctuous – just a little more salt and a splash of that aged vinegar will help bind it and sharpen it up.

I swiftly shake and tumble the chard through its pan, then drop the spuds onto our plates with a slash, a squeeze and a big knob of butter. The excess juices from the chard save our reducing sauce, then I make a loose nest of the leaves and stalks, squeezing every last drop of sauce over the top through a small strainer. I grab my knife and take to the legs in a ravenous frenzy, peeling each off the bone after one central cut. In mere moments, no one can interrupt!

In all the excitement I've forgotten about my rendering pot, pushed to the back of the stove. It's nicely swollen, with all the brown bits of crisp skin floating on the top. Knowing of my rather scary, ever-growing supply of fat in the fridge, this pot begs to be tampered with, so I'm going to make cakes – of soap!

After a tip through the strainer, I bulk up the fat with a dollop from that surplus to make half a kilo. I have a quarter-cup of caustic soda flakes on hand and a cup of rainwater, straight from the tap. Rosemary oil seems like a logical fragrance and six tiny tart shells will be perfect for moulds . . .

First up, I set all the fat to warm slowly, resting a thermometer evenly in the middle, to hover between 35 and 38 degrees. I spread out a couple of layers of newspaper, then rub a thin film of Vaseline inside the tins.

I sit a pot in the sink with the rainwater inside and surrounded by cold water for cooling, then find a suitable stirring stick. I open the window wide for fresh air, too hasty for goggles or gloves. Once the fat's up to temp, I stir the caustic flakes into the rainwater and bring in the thermometer to make sure both are pretty much around the same mark. I pour my toxic water slowly into the fat, as though making mayonnaise, stirring and stirring . . . After surely 20 minutes has passed, my 'mayo' finally thickens; at last, I can beat in my fragrance and fill up my moulds.

I need to wait at least a day, sometimes several, for the cakes to set enough to slip out of their tins. Then, resting on well-ventilated slats, they are left to mature for at least a month.

For a final touch, I buff my freshly scented cakes with a towel until they're shiny and gleaming – like I soon will be!

Quail Salad with Figs, Pancetta and Radicchio

What I love about quail, particularly what are known in the market as jumbo quail, is that they have the perfect ratio of body fat to meat. Whether grilled over coals (backbone snipped away and meat flattened) or roasted and rested, the resulting succulence never disappoints.

While it's preferable to use a properly reduced game stock here, you can make a dainty little stock with the quail trimmings. In this case, you caramelise the trimmings, livers and hearts in oil or duck fat, then grate in ½ onion, ½ carrot and ½ stick celery, along with a couple of minced cloves of garlic, a bay leaf and a small handful of parsley stalks. The red wine from the currants is used to deglaze the pan, then the lot is just covered with cold water and simmered for 20–40 minutes until reduced as required.

This warm salad makes an ideal entrée or light lunch, particularly in early autumn when figs are at their best. Choose soft figs, keeping in mind that they will only ripen on the tree. Hearts of radicchio nicely 'cup' the stuffing – inspired by the legendary Janni Kyritsis and his famous barley stuffing – and the twig-like snake-beans are, perhaps, remnants of a nest . . .

SERVES **6**

6 jumbo quail

75 ml extra-virgin olive oil

12 paper-thin slices flat pancetta

salt and freshly ground black pepper

10 thin snake beans

6 ripe figs

2 heads radicchio (preferably long-leafed Treviso)

2 tablespoons walnut oil

1 tablespoon good-quality red-wine vinegar

2 tablespoons reduced Game Stock (see page 191)

1 clove garlic

1 pinch castor sugar (optional)

STUFFING

100 g coarse cracked wheat

salt

2 tablespoons currants

2 tablespoons red wine

½ teaspoon cumin seeds

1 large onion

2 cloves garlic

1 handful sage leaves

⅓ cup extra-virgin olive oil

2 tablespoons pine nuts

finely grated zest of 1 lemon

freshly ground black pepper

1   To make the stuffing, bring 300 ml water to a boil over a moderate flame in a small, heavy-based saucepan, then stir in cracked wheat and a generous pinch of salt. Cover and lower heat, then simmer gently for about 15–20 minutes, stirring occasionally, until all water has been absorbed and wheat is tender (you may need to use a simmer mat). Leave cracked wheat in pan for several minutes, still covered, then pour onto a tray or into a wide bowl to cool.

2   Meanwhile, soak currants in red wine. In a small frying pan, toast cumin seeds over a low flame until fragrant, then cool and grind. Peel and roughly dice onion. Peel and mince garlic. Coarsely chop sage leaves.

3   Heat extra-virgin olive oil in a wide frying pan over a moderate flame, then sauté onion and pine nuts until golden, stirring frequently. Add minced garlic, sage and ground cumin and sauté for several seconds before mixing in cracked wheat, lemon zest and soaked currants with a drizzle of their soaking liquor. Season to taste and remove from heat to cool.

4 Preheat oven to 200°C. Using a sharp pair of kitchen scissors, snip quail wings down to about 1 cm from where bone meets breast meat, just below each joint – this enables the quail to sit flatter in the pan and colour up more evenly. (For serving in the restaurant we also cut the knuckles from the tips of the legs – merely a professional 'dress', providing a more 'polite' handle for the diner, so suit yourself.) Pull out hearts and gizzards, then dry skin and cavity with paper towel. Divide stuffing between the birds, pushing well into cavities.

5 Meanwhile, heat half the extra-virgin olive oil over moderate heat in an ovenproof frying pan wide enough to fit quail comfortably. Pan-fry pancetta on each side until deep golden, then lift onto paper towel and keep warm. Lay quail in pan on their sides, then season well with salt and pepper and turn after several moments when nicely golden. Season reverse side of birds, then slide into hot oven to roast for 9 minutes. Remove and rest for at least 20 minutes before carving.

6 Blanch snake beans in boiling salted water until tender, then drain and refresh in cold water to room temperature (the beans tend to discolour and overcook if this isn't done). Cut each bean into about 10 cm lengths, trimming away tough ends. Trim twig ends from figs. Remove and discard core and outer leaves from radicchio, then separate hearts, choosing leaves about same size as snake beans.

7 Make a dressing by whisking remaining extra-virgin olive oil, walnut oil, vinegar, game stock, lightly crushed garlic clove and all juices from resting quail, then season to taste (a sprinkling of sugar helps round off flavours). Keep warm.

8 To assemble, scoop stuffing from each bird into a large bowl. Tear or cut each fig into quarters and put into bowl with radicchio leaves and snake beans. Using a sharp, small paring knife, cut legs from quail by following natural line of meat, curving knife to free tiny 'oyster' of meat from underneath. Double check insides of legs are free from all surface bone, leaving only one central leg bone holding meat. Starting at pointy end of each bird, remove breasts, cutting slightly off-centre to avoid breast bone and following backbone down carefully, then cut between wishbone and wing joint. Add boned quail meat to bowl (save or freeze carcasses for making stock later), then drizzle with dressing and season. Toss salad gently before 'nesting' on a central platter or on individual plates and scattering with crumbled pancetta.

Spatchcock Fried in a Chickpea Crust, with Beans and Coleslaw

This recipe can be doubled (or tripled) successfully, depending mainly on the size of your deep-fryer, so, Colonel Sanders, eat your heart out! Just remember to start preparations the day before you want to tuck in as the beans need to soak overnight.

SERVES 2

100 g dried cannellini or haricot beans

2 × 500 g spatchcocks

2 heaped teaspoons fine salt

2 cloves garlic

1 bay leaf

100 ml extra-virgin olive oil

6 litres sunflower or olive oil

1 teaspoon cumin seeds

½ cup chickpea flour

1 teaspoon mild Spanish paprika

1 teaspoon dried chilli powder (optional)

freshly ground black pepper

1 egg white

COLESLAW

100 g green cabbage

100 g red cabbage

1 small carrot

1 stick celery

2 spring onions

1 apple (preferably golden delicious)

2 radishes

50 ml white-wine vinegar

1 teaspoon castor sugar

salt

125 ml Mayonnaise (see page 196)

freshly ground black pepper

1   The day before you plan to eat, soak beans in triple their volume of cool water and prepare spatchcocks. Pull all excess fat globules from inside spatchcocks. Using a sharp pair of kitchen scissors, snip away just below the first joint of each wing tip. Trim excess neck and neck skin, then remove wishbones by scraping flesh with a knife and pulling free. (Add trimmings to poultry bone supply in freezer.) Season each bird all over with fine salt, making sure you reach under wings and between legs, then refrigerate, covered, overnight.

2   Next day, drain beans and put into a suitably small pan with 1½ times their volume of fresh, cool water, then add peeled garlic cloves and bay leaf and bring to a boil. Reduce heat and simmer for 1½ hours, uncovered, until tender, then drain. Discard bay leaf, then season to taste and drizzle with extra-virgin olive oil. Leave to cool to room temperature.

3   Meanwhile, make coleslaw. Discard any core from both pieces of cabbage, then shred cabbage finely. Peel carrot, then cut into matchstick lengths or push carefully through a mandoline and add to cabbage. Strip 'string' from celery and discard, then cut into similar lengths. Trim spring onions and repeat matchstick cut. Peel and core apple, then cut likewise. Grate radishes. Toss vegetables with vinegar, sugar and a generous sprinkling of salt, then place in a fine-meshed strainer for about 15 minutes while frying spatchcocks.

4   Heat sunflower or olive oil to 160°C in a deep-fryer or in a very large pan (at least 10-litre capacity) – use a thermometer. Meanwhile, toast cumin seeds in a small frying pan over a low flame until fragrant, then cool and grind. Mix ground cumin, chickpea flour, paprika and chilli powder (if using) and add several twists from the pepper mill. Lightly whisk egg white. Dust each spatchcock all over with spiced flour, including inside cavity. Holding legs (so you don't smear off flour) and using a pastry brush, paint birds entirely with egg white and dust again with spiced flour. Gently lower birds into hot oil, ensuring they are fully submerged, and fry for 9 minutes. Remove from oil to paper towel, then increase heat to 180°C and leave birds to rest for at least 10 minutes.

5   Just before you are ready to serve, squeeze excess moisture from coleslaw firmly with your hands, then repeat. Toss with mayonnaise and add a twist or two of pepper. Crisp spatchcocks by refrying for a mere 10 seconds, then drain on paper towel, carefully tipping out any oil trapped inside, and present alongside beans and coleslaw.

CHICKEN
PICKEN'S

Good Chook, Roasted with Oregano, with Creamed Corn

Don't be deceived by a label that boasts a wholesome chook to be 'corn-fed'; the yellow tinge of the skin is testament to that. Most corn-fed chooks are pumped up on layer pellets as well, and spend their life tightly caged.

By good chook, I mean a chook that has foraged on natural, grassed runs, free to scrape here and there for worms and bugs. Their diet has been balanced by the provision of various GM-free grains, handfuls of vegetable scraps, weeds, and a few well-crushed egg shells for essential grit. Therefore, this is a diet free from preservatives, drugs or growth hormones. By choosing a plump, quality, free-range bird as opposed to any old battery hen, you will not only delight in the unsurpassed flavour but embrace this harmonious, holistic life-cycle passed on from chook to egg.

I prefer to 'wet-roast' my chook in the Italian manner, lemon inside and trussed in the old-fashioned, stringless way, so that the bird neatly hugs itself, retaining all its juices. I also like to add a dab of tomato paste to the stock before pouring it over the bird to roast, for an even more appetising bloom – and the wafting aroma of the oregano-infused duck fat really gets me salivating!

SERVES **4**

6 cloves garlic

2 generous handfuls oregano

salt

freshly ground black pepper

2 heaped tablespoons duck fat *or* butter

1 × 1.8–2 kg free-range chook

1 lemon

8 salad onions

1 teaspoon tomato paste

500 ml Chook Stock (see page 191)

250 ml dry white wine

CREAMED CORN

½ teaspoon cumin seeds

1 large onion

1 clove garlic

4 cobs corn

50 ml olive oil

6 sprigs thyme

150 ml dry white wine

250 ml Chook Stock (see page 191)

salt

freshly ground black pepper >

1 Peel 2 of the cloves of garlic and pick oregano leaves, then grind to a smooth paste in a mortar and pestle with a generous pinch of salt and a few twists of pepper. Mix duck fat through paste.

2 With legs of the chook pointing towards you, slip your fingers under the breast skin to free it from the flesh, pushing carefully all the way down to the wing-bone joint on both sides, then slide seasoned fat in under the skin, being careful not to puncture it as you go. Cut lemon in half and squeeze as you insert each half inside cavity of chook. Pull breast skin tightly towards you and make a small incision at the central point, about 1 cm in from the top of cavity, then tuck the end of each drumstick through this hole so that the legs cross. At the other end of the bird, tuck any excess neck skin underneath and twist each wing tip back and under for support in the baking dish.

3 Trim onions, leaving on 3–4 cm of green stalk, then peel. Whisk tomato paste with a little stock until smooth, then stir in remaining stock.

4 Preheat oven to 200°C. Pour wine into a suitably large, heavy-based baking dish and add onions. Sit chook in dish, breast-side up, then pour stock mixture over bird and season well. Roast for 20 minutes, then turn bird onto its side and return to oven for another 20 minutes. Turn bird again for a final 20 minutes, adding remaining unpeeled garlic cloves to dish. Remove from oven and rest for 20–30 minutes. Leave oven on.

5 While the chook is roasting, make the creamed corn. In a small dry frying pan, toast cumin seeds over a low flame until fragrant, then cool and grind. Peel onion and chop roughly. Peel and crush garlic. Strip ears and silk from corn and cut kernels away from cob by running a sharp cook's knife down sides, being careful to avoid any tough husk.

6 Heat oil in a small, heavy-based pan over a moderate flame and sauté onion for several minutes until lightly caramelised. Add corn, ground cumin, garlic and thyme (stalks and all), then sauté for several more minutes until sugars just start to catch on base of pan. Deglaze with wine and stock, then reduce heat and cook at a steady simmer for 20–30 minutes, stirring occasionally, until corn is tender. Remove from heat and allow to cool slightly, then discard thyme sprigs. Set aside a large spoonful of corn, then blend remaining corn for a couple of minutes. Pass through a sieve or the coarse blade of a Mouli, then return saved corn and season well to taste. Keep warm or reheat for serving under chook.

7 Just before carving, pick out onions and garlic cloves from chook dish and return to oven to glaze on a baking tray for a few minutes. I like to carve the chook in the roasting dish so I catch all the juices. Remove carcass, squeezing juice from lemon halves into pan (discard lemons but keep carcass for making stock). Gently spoon excess fat from baking dish, then quickly reduce over a full flame to a saucing consistency and check seasoning.

8 Serve carved chook at once on a bed of creamed corn with the crisp garlic cloves and onions, a roasted potato or two and a leafy green salad.

Guinea Fowl Roasted with Chestnut, Sultana and Thyme Stuffing

Despite the fact our finest guinea fowl bear little resemblance to the plump, golden-fleshed beauties of European hill towns, a well-bred fowl can be a fantastic eating bird. Being the leanest of game birds, its flesh needs a resting period of at least several days after slaughter to help tenderise it and increase its fine flavour. Then it's the cook's responsibility to compensate for the leanness by wrapping the bird in bacon or pancetta or sliding some fat under the skin.

A characteristic toughening of fibres in the drumsticks of guinea fowl, more obvious to the eye in pheasant, can sometimes disappoint. The fibres can be removed prior to cooking by running a knife around the top section of drumstick meat and pulling the fibres free with pliers, or simply by cutting between the thigh joint when serving – I tend not to serve the drumstick in the restaurant, but am rather partial to its more fibrous texture for private snacking.

Guinea fowl are at their best in autumn, along with chestnuts, just as the nip in the air makes us hanker for richer flavours. After the initial fuss, I think a stuffing like this pays an appropriate compliment. I reckon this dish is perfect with Brussels Sprouts Sautéed with Garlic and Sage (see page 49) and a few crunchy potatoes roasted in duck fat.

SERVES 2

1 handful flat-leaf parsley

1 clove garlic

salt

3 heaped tablespoons duck fat *or* butter

1 × 900 g–1 kg free-range guinea fowl

1 handful thyme sprigs

250 ml reduced Game or Chook Stock (see page 191)

1 tablespoon red-wine vinegar

freshly ground black pepper

1 pinch castor sugar (optional)

STUFFING

100 g chestnuts

1 large onion

2 cloves garlic

1 handful thyme sprigs

2 heaped tablespoons duck fat *or* olive oil

50 ml dry white wine

1 heaped tablespoon sultanas

finely grated zest of 1 orange

⅔ cup coarse fresh breadcrumbs

salt

freshly ground black pepper

1 Make the stuffing. Using a small, sharp knife, make a little criss-cross incision at the fatter end of each chestnut. Bring a small saucepan of water to a boil, then blanch nuts for several minutes, removing each nut one at a time into a clothed palm to peel, stripping away both outer tough and inner furry skins. This is much easier to achieve while the nuts are as hot as possible. Chop chestnuts or pulse in a food processor to make coarse crumbs about 2 mm in size. >

2   Peel and finely chop onion. Peel garlic, then strip thyme leaves from stalks and chop together finely. Heat duck fat or olive oil in a small to medium frying pan over a moderate flame, then sauté onion for several minutes until lightly caramelised. Add garlic, thyme and chestnuts and continue sautéing until just starting to brown and catch, then deglaze pan with wine. Add sultanas, orange zest and breadcrumbs, then season well and remove from heat to cool.

3   Wash parsley, then dry and pick leaves from stems. Pound peeled garlic with parsley leaves and a generous sprinkling of salt to a smooth paste in a mortar and pestle, then mix in 2 tablespoons of the duck fat or butter.

4   Dry bird inside and out with paper towel. With the legs of the bird pointing towards you, slip your fingers under the breast skin to free it from the flesh, pushing carefully all the way down to the wing-bone joint on both sides, then slide seasoned fat or butter in under the skin, being careful not to puncture it. Fill cavity with stuffing and 'sew' opening together with a toothpick. Pull breast skin tightly towards you and cut a small incision at the central point, about 1 cm in from the top of cavity, then tuck the end of each drumstick through this hole so that the legs cross. At the other end of the bird, tuck any excess neck skin underneath and twist each wing tip back and under for support.

5   Preheat oven to 220°C. Strip thyme leaves from stalks. Heat remaining duck fat or butter over a moderate flame in an ovenproof frying pan that just fits bird. Carefully lay guinea fowl on its side in pan, then season well and sprinkle with half the thyme leaves. Sauté for several moments until skin is golden. Repeat this step on other side, using remaining thyme. Slide pan into oven and roast bird for 10 minutes on one side, then for 10 minutes on the other. Remove legs (thighs attached) from bird (leaving breast meat on) and pour stock into pan. Set carcass with breast meat aside somewhere warm and return legs to pan, skin-side up. Roast legs for about 4 minutes until juice from thickest part of thigh runs clear when tested with a skewer. Remove from oven and rest for at least 20 minutes with breast meat.

6   To serve, scoop stuffing onto plates or a platter before removing breasts from carcass with a sharp knife. Scrape all juices from carving and resting platters into baking dish with vinegar, then reduce to a saucing consistency over a moderate flame and season to taste. A sprinkling of castor sugar may be needed to round off flavours. Arrange legs and breast meat on a bed of stuffing and mask with sauce.

Manoo's Eggs

toast and lift out the bacon – I drain all the excess fat back into the pan before lying them alongside. Like Manoo, I throw the onions into the pan, turn off the jet, swiftly grab the wooden spoon and pour in the eggs. With a swirl of the pan I scrape all the caught bits in four persuasive movements. This 'cleaning of the pan' is what makes these eggs all the more Manoo's. He's one of those rare, dream cooks who washes up meticulously as they go.

This is what I adore most about home cookin'!

Ironically, it's Easter Sunday and our three-year-old nephew has just popped around with a handful of shiny eggs for us, and a cake he baked for the chooks!

Manoo's chooks are almost as endearing as Manoo's Eggs. This morning I've noticed a couple of young onions he's obviously pulled from the garden lying on top of a bowl with 5 eggs. It's a subtle hint. There's bacon in the fridge and day-old bread for toast, so, this time, his treat's on me.

I grab his favourite large, non-stick pan and click on the gas. I crack the eggs into a bowl then give 'em a loose whisk. I remember a few twists of pepper is all that's needed. No salt, no butter, no cream.

Now the pan is hot enough for the rashers, so I lay in all four, almost as neatly as Manoo would. The onions need a snip of the roots, a peel and a rinse before a rough slice, then the bacon spits at me for attention. After a turn of each rasher, I salivate and bung on the toast. Within no time the bacon is crisp and there are those usual tasty, caramelised blobs congealing around the pan. Now's the time to plate up the

119

Milk-fed Lamb Roasted with Tuscan Chunks, and Mashed Peas

Ask your butcher to find lamb fed exclusively on milk, checking that the diet of the ewe is free from all drugs and hormones. At 5–8 weeks old, milk-fed lambs generally weigh 6–10 kg from May to December, then up to 16 kg by February. Don't confuse 'milk-fed' with 'spring lamb': sometimes sold as milk-fed, the red-branded 'springs' are anything from 10 months to 2 years old, with the flavour and colour of their meat deepening with time and diet.

Unless you intend to spit-roast your milk-fed lamb whole, it may be wise to ask your butcher to bone it into individual joints when you place your order. You'll then end up with two legs, two shoulders, a saddle, two racks (with chine bones removed for easier carving) and, if you're lucky, a set of kidneys. Be sure the butcher saves you all the bones for the stock you need to make.

'Tuscan chunks' are simply chunks of potato roasted in my favourite rustic Italian manner – infused with rosemary and with well-crisped garlic cloves, skins on and slightly crushed. Minted, mashed peas make the perfect, traditional accompaniment. Unless you've just picked your own, I thoroughly recommend using frozen peas for this recipe, as even day-old 'fresh' peas don't give the same vibrant results.

I can't resist the young, delectable milk-fed lamb available from reputable farms in the Barossa Valley or on Flinders Island. The meat is pale, sweet and extremely tender.

SERVES 12

3 heads garlic

6 large sprigs rosemary

1 milk-fed lamb (boned to individual joints)

2 kg roasting potatoes (sebago or russet burbanks, for example)

olive oil

salt

freshly ground black pepper

250 ml dry white wine

1 litre Lamb Stock (see below)

1 tablespoon tomato paste

2 tablespoons balsamic vinegar

MASHED PEAS

⅓ teaspoon cumin seeds

2 large onions

1 clove garlic

225 ml olive oil

500 ml dry white wine

1 kg frozen peas

200 ml water

1 tablespoon castor sugar

1 handful mint leaves

salt

freshly ground black pepper

1   The day before you plan to eat, peel and coarsely crush 1 of the heads of garlic. Pick ¾ of the rosemary leaves from the stalks and coarsely chop. Rub garlic and rosemary all over jointed lamb, then cover with plastic film and refrigerate overnight. Meanwhile, make a stock using the saved lamb bones and by following the instructions for Chook, Game, Veal or Beef Stock on page 191 and leave to simmer overnight. >

2   The next day, preheat oven to 200°C. Cut unpeeled potatoes into large, bite-sized cubes. Pour olive oil into a baking dish to a depth of 2 mm, then roll potato around in it before seasoning well with salt and pepper and sliding dish into oven for 20 minutes. Meanwhile, separate remaining garlic cloves, leaving the skins on, and pick remaining rosemary leaves from stalks. Using a fish slice, toss potato, scraping well from bottom of tray, and return to oven for a further 15 minutes. Scatter in garlic cloves, then toss with potato and return to oven for 6 minutes. Remove from oven, sprinkle over rosemary, then toss again and leave for reheating later. Leave oven on.

3   Choose 2 baking dishes large enough to accommodate all joints comfortably. Line each dish with a thin layer of olive oil, then stand them over a full flame. When hot, carefully lower in each piece of lamb, skin-side down, with the larger legs and shoulders in one dish and the racks, saddle and kidneys in the other. Season well. Turn each piece over when deep golden and swiftly season again. Transfer dishes to hot oven and cook for the following times: kidneys 8 minutes; racks 12 minutes; saddle 15 minutes; shoulders 20 minutes and legs 30 minutes. As each piece is cooked, remove from oven and keep warm, tipping fat directly from dish onto potato. Leave oven on.

4   While the meat is resting, make the mashed peas. In a small dry frying pan, toast cumin seeds over a low flame until fragrant, then cool and grind. Peel and cut onions into rough dice. Peel and crush garlic. Heat olive oil in a saucepan and sauté onion until lightly caramelised. Add garlic, wine, peas, water, castor sugar and ground cumin, and continue cooking gently for about 15 minutes, stirring frequently. Add mint leaves, then remove from heat and purée using a food processor or hand-held blender, and season to taste. Keep warm.

5   While the peas are cooking, make the sauce. Stand one of the baking dishes over a moderate flame and pour in wine and lamb stock to deglaze, rubbing congealed juices well with a wooden spoon, then remove from heat. Stand other dish over flame and deglaze with juices from first pan. Add tomato paste, vinegar and any juices from resting joints. Simmer to a saucing consistency, then check seasoning and strain. Keep sauce warm while carving the lamb.

6   Return potato to oven for 8–10 minutes for a final crisp while carving lamb. The most awkward joint to carve is the shoulder, with its slightly triangular bone structure hidden inside, so stick as close to the bone as you can. The rest is fairly straightforward. Cut lengthways down the saddle, slightly off-centre, to remove loins on each side (about 2 cm in diameter and 10 cm long), then slice it diagonally. Turn saddle over to remove the tiny fillet that you will be able to feel with your fingers. Slice cutlets off from top to bottom, using each bone as a guide for your knife. As you cut through the leg, try to change angles with each muscle so that you are cutting against the grain (basically, if the meat appears striped, carve the other way). Be sure not to forget the kidneys – simply split the pair and serve to your favourite or discreetly eat them all yourself!

7   Scrape any tasty juices from your chopping board into the sauce, then quickly reheat it in a small saucepan. Serve lamb and its sauce on mashed peas with crisped potatoes and, perhaps, some steamed asparagus.

Veal Scaloppine, Pan-fried with Sage and Pancetta, with Borlotti Bean Purée

The varying shades of veal are often the best indicator of the subtleties one can expect to experience when eating this meat, from the slightly embryonic flavour of a 'bobby' calf to the tastier, darker flesh of a grass-muncher from the pristine pastures on King Island. Pale, delicate and buttery milk-fed veal, such as our lauded benchmark White Rocks veal from Western Australia, is hard to resist.

For superior veal scaloppine, choose meat from the legs of milk-fed calves. It is essential to cut slices from individual muscles, running across the grain, so be sure to check there is no visible 'striping' in the veal you purchase from your butcher.

SERVES **4–6**

200 ml extra-virgin olive oil

8 × 5 mm thick milk-fed veal scaloppine (about 650 g)

plain flour, for dusting

8 paper-thin slices flat pancetta

12 large sage leaves

salt

freshly ground black pepper

200 ml dry white wine

2 tablespoons balsamic vinegar

BORLOTTI BEAN PURÉE

1 kg borlotti beans in the pod *or* 200 g dried borlotti beans, soaked overnight and drained

⅓ teaspoon cumin seeds

juice of 1 lemon

1 clove garlic

200 ml extra-virgin olive oil

¼ cup boiling water

salt

freshly ground black pepper

1   To make the borlotti bean purée, shell beans and discard pods. Cover beans with double their volume of cold water and bring to a boil, then reduce heat and simmer until tender, about 30 minutes (or 1–2 hours for dried beans). Meanwhile, in a small dry frying pan, toast cumin seeds over a low flame until fragrant, then cool and grind. Strain beans, then purée in a blender with lemon juice, garlic and ground cumin while drizzling in oil followed by the boiling water. Season to taste and keep warm.

2   Heat half the extra-virgin olive oil in a frying pan large enough to accommodate veal in one layer. Dust veal with flour and swiftly shake off excess. Sauté pancetta on each side in pan until golden, then drain on paper towel. Add sage leaves to pan and fry for a second or two until translucent and crisp, then add to pancetta. When pan is back to full heat, carefully lower in slices of veal and swiftly season, then turn and repeat for several seconds until lightly golden. Transfer to a warm plate to relax for a minute or two. Meanwhile, deglaze pan with wine and vinegar over a full flame. Add remaining oil, tip in all juices from rested veal and simmer to a saucing consistency.

3   Arrange scaloppine on top of bean purée and mask with sauce. Scatter with crisped pancetta and sage and serve with a salad or favoured green vegetable.

Beef Brisket, Braised, with Field Mushrooms in Mustard Sauce

Brisket is basically the breast of the cow and has a uniquely stringy texture. Don't let this put you off. I remember serving an interesting salad with lengths of finely torn brisket 'string' at Gay Bilson's Berowra Waters Inn back in 1983. We tossed through slivers of cornichon, pickled walnuts and herbs before dressing the lot with the stock infused with lemon zest.

But braising is where brisket comes into its own. The gutsy flavours of slowly braised brisket are extremely seductive. You can braise the piece whole (up to 40 cm long) or ask your butcher for the double-layered 'point end' connected by fat – the fat melts during cooking, basting the meat beautifully. As an experiment recently I braised Wagyu brisket, which has almost as much fat marbling as meat, with dangerously addictive results!

SERVES 4–6

2 onions

3 large carrots

2 sticks celery

1 sprig rosemary

5 cloves garlic

salt

1 × 1 kg piece of brisket (preferably 'point end')

olive oil

freshly ground black pepper

2 litres Beef Stock (see page 191)

250 ml red wine

100 ml red-wine vinegar

2 bay leaves

2 handfuls flat-leaf parsley leaves

finely grated zest of 1 lemon

12 large field mushrooms

2 tablespoons Dijon mustard

1   Preheat oven to 150°C. Peel and roughly chop onions. Peel and thinly slice carrots and roughly slice celery. Pick rosemary leaves from stalk and roughly chop. Peel and mince 4 of the garlic cloves with 1 tablespoon salt. Trim brisket of excess surface fat and carefully slide a sharp knife under any silver sinew and discard.

2   Heat 100 ml olive oil over a moderate flame in a large, heavy-based baking dish (preferably enamelled cast-iron). Add brisket and seal until golden brown on all sides. Season with salt and pepper. Brown onion, carrot and celery (remove brisket to make room, if necessary). When nicely caramelised, deglaze dish with stock, wine and vinegar and add rosemary, garlic paste and bay leaves and bring to a boil. Return meat to dish, if appropriate. Scrunch up a sheet of baking paper, then drench it with cold water to weigh it down and tuck it in around meat (the paper should sit down over the meat and fit the pan snugly – this technique prevents too much evaporation). Slide dish into oven to simmer for 2½–4 hours until brisket is tender all the way along – test for tenderness with a cook's fork or metal skewer: it should slide through the meat with ease. (The cooking time is difficult to pinpoint as it largely depends on the thickness of the brisket – the double-layered point end takes longer.)

3   Using a fish slice in one hand and a pair of tongs in the other, carefully remove brisket to a large platter or tray. Cut meat across grain into 2–3 cm thick slices, then strain stock, discarding 'solids'. The sliced brisket can be left to cool in the stock before being refrigerated – it will keep (all the better) this way for at least a week.

4   Ten minutes before serving, make gremolata by mincing remaining garlic clove with parsley and lemon zest. Heat the same baking dish over a moderate flame with a little olive oil. Sauté thickly sliced mushrooms until golden on both sides, seasoning well with salt and pepper as you go. Add sliced brisket, mustard and about a third of the strained stock. Shake pan gently to help amalgamate mustard and stock, then reduce to a saucing consistency. You can adjust the sauce with more stock if needed, otherwise any excess stock can be recycled or frozen. Check seasoning.

5   Serve the brisket with the mushrooms and sauce sprinkled with gremolata, and with a few boiled potatoes and perhaps some sautéed spinach or other greens alongside.

Skirt Steak, Marinated and Seared Rare

Skirt steak is cut off the flank, down around the crotch of the cow. Extremely full of flavour, the much-neglected whole skirt (weighing on average 800–900 g) is also inexpensive. About 45 cm long, the skirt is roughly 1 cm thick at one end (this is known as the 'flat') and then doubles in size two-thirds of the way along to become 'thick', at which point there is a notable change in the grain. To aid even cooking, these two sections need to be prised apart with your fingers and a knife where the connective tissue joins them. As it is well marbled, the skirt is best suited to being marinated for a long time before being seared over high heat and rested for several minutes then sliced thinly.

The following recipe is based on one from *City Cuisine* by Los Angeles restaurant cooks Susan Feniger and Mary Sue Milliken. This book was given to me by Anders Ousback, and my version of the dish subsequently became a staple at Taylor Square Restaurant when I was there in the 1980s. I have omitted the mustard powder used in the original, and swapped Tabasco for fresh chilli. If I'm using the more highly marbled grain-fed Wagyu beef, I also reduce the amount of olive oil from 250 ml to 2 tablespoons.

SERVES **4–6**

1 whole skirt steak (800–900 g)

2 cloves garlic

1–2 bird's-eye chillies

250 ml olive oil

2 tablespoons red-wine vinegar

2 tablespoons Worcestershire sauce

125 ml soy sauce

1 generous handful thyme leaves

1 teaspoon freshly ground black pepper

1   Prepare skirt for marinating by carefully trimming away any silvery sinew, leaving all fat attached, then separate 'thin' from 'thick' as described above. Put pieces of skirt into a glass or ceramic dish.

2   To make the marinade, peel and mince garlic and finely chop chilli, scraping away seeds if desired. Mix garlic and chilli with remaining ingredients, then tip over beef. With gloved hands, massage beef well with marinade. Cover meat and leave to marinate overnight or, preferably, for 2 days, refrigerated. Turn the meat in the marinade from time to time.

3   When ready to serve, preheat a barbecue hotplate or a large, heavy-based frying pan. Pat skirt dry with paper towel. If grilling steak over coals, rub a little oil over meat. If cooking in a frying pan or on a hotplate, use 1 tablespoon olive oil (I tend to scoop a little off the top of the marinade, although beware as it tends to spit for a few moments until rid of excess moisture). Cook over a high heat for 1–1½ minutes on either side, then remove and rest for 8–10 minutes. While the meat is resting, bring marinade to a boil in a saucepan over a moderate flame. Slice beef across the grain into thin strips, arrange on warmed plates and drizzle with resting juices and a little warmed marinade. I like to serve skirt steak with boiled green beans and squashed fried potatoes – and a dark, sweet beer, such as stout.

Ye Olde Pork Rack, Roasted with Fennel Seeds, Pumpkin and Pear, with Cabbage

Please don't be disillusioned with animal fat. Most of this highly *un*saturated lard will melt during cooking, helping to tenderise and enhance FLAVOUR.

Just in case you haven't already tasted the full flavour of hormone-free, highly marbled pork available in Australia under the 'Bangalow Sweet', 'Kurabuta' or 'Fine Swine' labels, just to name a few, La Dolce Vita Fine Foods, Nicholas Foods or Wrights the Butchers will happily sell you some (see page 212 for contact details). You will then discover that there is no comparison with the lean, mean, supermarket offerings that many of us are too often deeply dissatisfied with.

Ask your butcher to remove the chine bone for ease of carving and keep it for making stock. Unless you specify otherwise, they may automatically trim the flavoursome meat between each cutlet in your rack for presentation, leaving a polite, clean bone to hold for gnawing. This is known in the trade as 'frenching' – if a frenched cutlet is your preference, make sure you keep the highly prized belly meat to braise, for example, in a hearty soup.

It is possible to remove the skin on a rack for 'crackling' first, then trim off a few millimetres of excess creamy lard and save it for dishes using leaner cuts in need of moisture assistance, such as veal for meatballs, or even a lard pastry. I have included details at the start of this recipe if this is your preference and you have the extra time. However, the dish works equally well if the skin is left in place.

After roasting, the fat phobic among us will want to drain off the dissolved excess – seen as a crime by flavour hedonists like myself. After all, there is cabbage to sauté and pumpkin and potatoes to roast . . .

SERVES 6

1 × 6-cutlet, well-marbled rack of pork (chine bone removed)

4 cloves garlic

2 tablespoons fennel seeds

1 tablespoon white vinegar

salt

800 g Queensland blue pumpkin

olive oil (optional)

freshly ground black pepper

3 ripe pears (preferably Josephine or Doyenné du comice)

juice of ½ lemon

500 ml dry white wine

½ Savoy cabbage

12 cavolo nero leaves

500 ml Veal Stock (see page 191)

red-wine vinegar (optional)

1 If you want to cook your crackling separately, preheat oven to 180°C. Using a sharp knife, carefully cut skin away from rack where it meets fat, leaving a thin film on underside. Put skin into a frying pan, then cover with cold water and bring to a boil. Refresh skin under cool water until at room temperature, then drain and pat dry with paper towel. Leaving a layer of about 7 mm fat on rack, trim away excess lard and store. Peel garlic cloves and crush to a paste with fennel seeds in a mortar and pestle. Score rack in horizontal lines, 1 cm apart and 5 mm deep, and push in paste. Score skin with a sharp knife every 2 cm, then make a paste with the vinegar and 2 tablespoons fine salt and rub over generously. Put skin (skin-side up) on a wire rack over a baking tray (for catching fat) and cook for 20–30 minutes until golden and evenly crackled. Give crackling a few taps to remove excess salt and keep warm. Leave oven on. >

2   Remove and discard seeds from pumpkin, then cut it into 6 pieces, skin on or off, as you like. In a small baking dish, melt about 200 g saved lard (if you're crackling the skin separately and have access to the fat) or add a splash of olive oil (if you have left the skin on and don't). Add pumpkin, season well and roast for 30–40 minutes until just tender and lightly browned. Meanwhile, peel and halve pears, and brush cut sides with lemon juice. Pour wine into a baking dish that will comfortably accommodate all pears and arrange them in it flat-side down. Scrunch up a sheet of baking paper and drench it with cold water to weigh it down before tucking it in around pears. Bake for 20–25 minutes, brushing exposed surfaces with cooking liquid a couple of times during cooking, until slightly translucent, then remove for glazing later. Turn pumpkin chunks when you remove the pears.

3   After removing pumpkin, increase the oven temperature to 200°C. If you have decided to leave the skin on your rack, prepare the crackling now by making the fennel paste as described above. Using a sharp knife, make several deep incisions along rack at regular intervals, through the skin and fat to just reach the meat. Push the fennel paste deeply into crevices to protect it from burning, then rub in the vinegar and fine salt paste, again as described above. Heat a heavy-based baking dish over a moderate flame, then carefully lower in rack, skin-side down. Leave for several minutes to spit and colour up nicely, adjusting flame and dish as needed.

4   Season rack (whether skin on or off), then slide into oven and roast for 50–60 minutes until juices run clear when meat is pierced with a cook's fork or metal skewer. Remove pork and leave to rest away from direct heat for 25–30 minutes. Spoon half the fat in the baking dish over the pumpkin pieces and the other half into a frying pan for the cabbage and cavolo nero. Put baking dish aside for deglazing later. Leave oven on.

5   Remove core from cabbage and cut into large bite-sized chunks. Wash cavolo nero leaves and strip each one from its stalk.

6   When you are ready to serve, drain excess liquid from pears into baking dish and return pears to hot oven with pumpkin for 5–8 minutes until deeply caramelised. Meanwhile, deglaze baking dish with stock over a moderate flame, rubbing well with a wooden spoon. Add juices drained from rack, then reduce to a saucing consistency and taste for seasoning – a few drops of red-wine vinegar will help balance and amalgamate sauce.

7   Swiftly sauté cabbage and cavolo nero over a moderate flame in frying pan with melted fat. Toss frequently until tender and season to taste, then set to carving pork. Lift crackling off rack, if necessary, and set aside. Using a large, sharp carving knife, cut bones off rear of rack by keeping knife flush with bones, then cut between each (this frees you up to carve meat as thinly as you like). Alternatively, cut rack into thick cutlets using each bone as a guide. Serve pork topped with crackling snapped into pieces and with pears, pumpkin and cabbage alongside.

Pork Neck Chops Braised with Anise, Shallots, Raisins and Sage

My favourite pork chop is cut from the neck of old-fashioned, well-marbled pigs like those described on page 131. Ask your butcher to cut the chops into generous 2 cm thick slices, allowing a chop per person, giving you more room in your baking tray. I like to accompany these luxuriously textured chops with stewed silver beet or colourful rainbow chard.

SERVES 6

400 g shallots

1 head garlic

2 handfuls sage

6 kipfler *or* pink-eye potatoes (about 500 g)

150 ml olive oil

6 × 2 cm thick pork neck chops (about 2.5 kg)

salt

freshly ground black pepper

500 ml dry white wine

1 litre Veal or Chook Stock (see page 191)

2 star anise, cloves *or* cinnamon sticks

150 g raisins

1 tablespoon balsamic vinegar

1   Preheat oven to 160°C. Blanch shallots in a small saucepan of boiling water for 1 minute, then refresh in cool water for several minutes before peeling. (Freeze skins for making fish stock another day.) Peel garlic and pick sage leaves from stems, then coarsely chop together. Peel and slice potatoes into 5 mm thick rounds.

2   Heat olive oil in a heavy-based baking dish large enough to hold chops in one layer. Carefully arrange chops in dish, then season well and sauté over a moderate flame until nicely caramelised on both sides. When chops are almost done, arrange shallots in gaps and sauté for several seconds before deglazing pan with wine and stock. Add star anise and potato, poking to submerge slices under stock, then scatter in raisins and the chopped garlic and sage. Scrunch up a sheet of baking paper before drenching it with cold water to weigh it down, then cover contents of dish snugly and bake for 1½–2 hours until tender.

3   Using a fish slice, carefully lift chops, potato, shallots and raisins onto plates or a serving platter and keep warm, discarding star anise as you find them. Add balsamic vinegar to baking dish, then reduce cooking liquid over a full flame for several minutes to a saucing consistency. Check seasoning. Meanwhile, prepare a green salad or sautéed silver beet or rainbow chard before serving with chops and sauce.

Slowly braised, these chops are slightly sweetened with raisins and shallots and spiced with star anise, cloves or cinnamon.

Vanilla Meringues with Strawberry Crush Ice-cream

I could say the great thing about this dessert is that it uses entire eggs. That could seem dull and irrelevant compared to the childish thrill of eating these lightly crusted meringues, which bleed with fragrant strawberry pulp and are filled with the sexiest strawberry ice-cream. Who really cares?

SERVES **4–6**

100 g pure icing sugar

1 teaspoon cornflour

1 vanilla bean

4 egg whites (from 60 g eggs at room temperature)

1 pinch fine salt

100 g castor sugar

1 teaspoon white vinegar

1 × 250 g punnet best strawberries

STRAWBERRY CRUSH ICE-CREAM

2 × 250 g punnets best strawberries

190 g castor sugar

375 ml pouring cream

4 egg yolks

1 Preheat oven to 100°C. Line a lightly greased baking tray with baking paper. Sift icing sugar with cornflour and scrape in seeds from split vanilla bean. Ensure the bowl of your electric mixer is scrupulously clean and dry before pouring in egg whites and salt. Whisk whites on full speed for several seconds, then gradually 'rain' in castor sugar. Continue beating until stiff peaks form, then gently fold in icing sugar mixture with vinegar. Using a large tablespoon, form 4–6 evenly spaced egg-shaped blobs on tray (peaks pointing nicely at the tops). Bake for 35 minutes, then switch off oven and leave meringues to cool inside.

2 To make the ice-cream, wash and hull strawberries, then mash with a third of the castor sugar until just coarsely puréed, and set aside. Bring cream to a boil over a moderate flame in a heavy-based saucepan. Have on hand a fine-meshed strainer and a large bowl with a layer of ice-cubes in it to cool custard swiftly the moment it's cooked. Meanwhile, whisk egg yolks with remaining castor sugar until pale, then pour in boiling cream. Whisk briefly, then return to pan over a low flame and cook, stirring constantly with a wooden spoon, until custard coats back of your spoon. It is imperative not to let the custard boil and scramble, yet it should congeal slightly at the base of the pan. Strain custard back into bowl, then stir in crushed strawberries and sit over ice to chill. When cold, churn in an ice-cream machine according to the manufacturer's instructions.

3 To serve, wash, hull and slightly crush the extra strawberries with a little icing sugar. Using a small, sharp, serrated knife, cut away the upper thin crusty shell of each meringue and gently lift it off. Scatter berries into meringues, then add a generous scoop of ice-cream and replace lids.

Chocolate Peanut Cookies

I always remember Franca Manfredi insisting that the secret to her extra-crisp and flavoursome crostoli was that she fried them in duck fat. Having a little extra duck fat on my hands of late, I've taken to substituting the lard for it in this old cookie recipe, which, until now, has been a big secret.

MAKES 33

¾ cup plain flour

¼ teaspoon baking powder

½ teaspoon salt

¼ cup duck fat, lard or butter

80 g softened unsalted butter

¾ cup firmly packed brown sugar

2 tablespoons castor sugar

1 vanilla bean

1 egg

3 teaspoons milk

1 cup rolled oats

1 cup unsalted peanuts

1 heaped cup best-quality dark chocolate buttons

1 Preheat oven to 160°C. Line 3 baking trays with baking paper. Combine flour, baking powder and salt in a bowl. Put duck fat, butter, brown sugar and castor sugar into bowl of an electric mixer, then scrape in seeds from split vanilla bean. Cream until thick and pale. Add egg and milk, then beat in flour mixture and oats. Fold in peanuts and chocolate buttons.

2 Using a tablespoon measure, scoop mixture, scraping top flush, and blob onto lined trays with 11 evenly spaced on each. Bake for 15 minutes, then remove to cool on a wire rack. Store in an airtight container.

Buttermilk Pancakes with Banana and Palm Treacle

I've included this recipe in memory of the crazy weekends we used to serve breakfast in the restaurant, and in honour of Nicola Flamer-Caldera, who first introduced me to the subtleties of kithul treacle extracted from the fish-tail palm, *Caryota urens*, of Sri Lanka. This irresistible caramel syrup is naturally sweet, not cloying like treacle.

A stack of these buttermilk pancakes layered with slices of the ripest banana and then smothered in syrup is a fun and healthy start to the day.

SERVES **4**

50 g unsalted butter

¼ cup rye flour

¼ cup wholemeal plain flour

¼ cup plain flour

1½ tablespoons fine polenta

1 heaped tablespoon castor sugar

2 scant teaspoons baking powder

¼ teaspoon bicarbonate of soda

1 teaspoon salt

2 eggs

300 ml buttermilk

4 ripe bananas

250 ml kithul treacle

1   Melt 35 g of the butter in a small saucepan and set aside. Sift all dry ingredients into a bowl and form a well in centre. Add eggs, buttermilk and melted butter and whisk slowly to form a smooth batter, then pour into a large jug.

2   Peel bananas and slice thinly lengthways into sixths, leaving them on your chopping board as you go. Heat a large, preferably non-stick frying pan over a moderate flame and arrange guests in a suitable eating order or, alternatively, warm a platter large enough to take the pancake stacks. Rub a small knob of butter around pan and, when foaming evenly, pour in about ¼ cup batter, then repeat twice more to give you 3 well-spaced pancakes (this is 1 serve). When you notice air holes forming evenly over surface after about a minute, carefully flip each pancake with a fish slice and cook for several seconds while you swiftly arrange 2 slices of banana on each. Stack pancakes, with banana in place, and serve immediately (or keep warm while you make the remaining pancakes) drizzled generously with treacle.

Apple and Blueberry Turnovers

The success of these addictive turnovers is partly due to Rose Levy Beranbaum's version in her meticulous *Pie and Pastry Bible*. Here the apple is leached of its juice, which is intensified by reduction, dusted with cornflour for the perfect 'sauce' and hugged by flaky cream-cheese pastry. We originally made her mini turnovers for our takeaway adjacent to the restaurant, combining the apple filling with blueberries for further texture and with a delightful deep-mauve 'stain' in mind. They are well worth the effort and can be frozen successfully, then thawed before baking.

MAKES **12**

4 golden delicious *or* Granny Smith apples

½ teaspoon ground cinnamon

115 g castor sugar

1 pinch salt

finely grated zest and juice of 1 lemon

30 g unsalted butter

1 level tablespoon cornflour

150 g blueberries

1 egg

1 tablespoon pouring cream

CREAM-CHEESE PASTRY

170 g chilled unsalted butter

125 g chilled cream cheese

285 g plain flour

1 pinch salt

¼ teaspoon baking powder

2 tablespoons iced water

1 tablespoon cider vinegar

1   Peel, core and cut apples into 5 mm dice (you should have 380 g diced fruit), then toss thoroughly with cinnamon, 100 g of the castor sugar, salt, lemon juice and zest. Tip apple mixture into a colander, then sit this over a large bowl and leave to leach for 2 hours, covered and refrigerated.

2   Meanwhile, make the pastry. Cut butter into 1 cm cubes and freeze for 30 minutes. Blend cream cheese, flour, salt and baking powder in a food processor until evenly grainy. Add chilled butter and pulse for several seconds until mixture is made up of pea-sized lumps – use a fork to check. Add iced water and vinegar and pulse for an extra second. Spoon mixture (which will be dry) into a freezer bag, then, holding both ends of bag with your fingers, knead from outside bag with heels and knuckles of your hands until dough holds together in one piece and feels slightly stretchy when pulled. Flatten dough into a disc and refrigerate, in the plastic bag, for at least 45 minutes.

3   Pour juices that have leached from apple into a small saucepan, then add butter and boil steadily over a moderate flame for several minutes to reduce to a thick saucing consistency. Remove from heat and leave to cool to room temperature.

4   Toss apple with cornflour, then add blueberries and cooled syrup and mix gently. Roll pastry out on a well-floured, clean workbench until 2 mm thick, then cut rounds with a 13 cm diameter pastry cutter (or cut around an upturned bowl).

5 Lightly beat and then strain egg. Brush excess flour from each pastry round, then divide apple filling between rounds, piling it onto one half and leaving a 1 cm edge. Paint edge lightly with egg before folding pastry over and pressing well to seal. Swiftly place each turnover onto a baking tray and refrigerate for at least 30 minutes before baking. Keep remaining egg.

6 Preheat oven to 180°C. Mix cream with remaining egg, then paint each turnover with this and dust with remaining castor sugar. Insert fork into centres to vent. Bake for 12–15 minutes until pastry is golden and filling is bubbling out the vents. Cool on a wire rack for 15 minutes before eating.

Apple Fritters with Spiced Grape Ice-cream

This ice-cream is simply the saviour of a sloppy batch of spiced grape jam. The hot/cold combination is an ideal sensation in winter – a generous scoop of luscious spicy ice-cream melting over fried, tart apples.

Handy hint no. 1: custard for ice-cream always needs to be chilled well before churning (unlike a fruit syrup for a sorbet) as unpleasant 'butter balls' (overbeaten fat) can form with too much churning. Handy hint no. 2: if you've saved spent vanilla beans by storing them in your castor sugar jar, you'll have beautifully perfumed vanilla sugar for dusting your fritters.

SERVES **4–6**

sunflower oil

3 large cooking apples (preferably Bramley or Granny Smith)

150 g plain flour

1 × 330 ml stubby of beer

150 g ice-cubes

1 tablespoon vanilla or castor sugar

SPICED GRAPE ICE-CREAM

1 vanilla bean

600 ml pouring cream

ice-cubes

6 egg yolks

200 g castor sugar

250 g Spiced Grape Jam
(see page 209)

1 To make the ice-cream, split vanilla bean and scrape seeds into cream in a heavy-based small saucepan and bring to a boil over a moderate flame. Have on hand a fine-meshed strainer and a large bowl with a layer of ice-cubes in it to cool custard swiftly the moment it's cooked. Meanwhile, whisk egg yolks with castor sugar until pale, then pour in boiling cream. Whisk briefly, then return to pan over a low flame and cook, stirring constantly with a wooden spoon, until custard coats back of your spoon. It is imperative not to let the custard boil and scramble, yet it should congeal slightly at the base of the pan. Strain custard back into bowl and sit over ice to chill. When cold, churn in an ice-cream machine according to the manufacturer's instructions, then fold through spiced grape jam and freeze for several hours to set.

2 Ten minutes before serving, fill a deep-fryer or suitably large pan with enough sunflower oil to fill just over halfway and heat to 190°C. Meanwhile, peel and core apples with an apple corer, then cut into 4 rings. Mix flour, beer and ice loosely together with a slotted spoon – there should be a few small lumps. Dip each apple ring into batter and drain excess, leaving just a film, then carefully lower into hot oil. Avoid overcrowding fryer as oil will lose heat and fritters will be soggy rather than crisp. Fry for several minutes and, after a turn to even up colour to a deep golden, remove to drain on paper towel. Keep warm until all are ready, or serve immediately, lightly dusted with vanilla sugar and topped with a dollop of ice-cream.

Keep a jar of vanilla sugar in your cupboard and simply rub through a sieve for fragrance beyond!

Rockmelon Ice-cream with Mint and Ginger Jewels

This ice-cream was inspired by an Alice Waters recipe for melon gelato, from her book *Chez Panisse Fruit*. The corn syrup she uses is a perfect stabiliser, preventing unwanted ice crystals. I like to stud my version with ginger 'jewels' and flecks of mint (particularly the pungent 'chocolate' mint). To highlight a contrasting terrazzo effect, I simmer the ginger in syrup with beetroot, which provides the perfect natural dye for my 'rubies', and serve this take on Italian cassata in its own natural bowl.

You end up with about a cup of leftover ginger jewels – they keep well and can also be used in a fruit compote or banana cake.

SERVES 4–6

350 g young ginger

1 beetroot

250 g castor sugar

ROCKMELON ICE-CREAM

1 perfectly ripe rockmelon

6 egg yolks

105 g castor sugar

150 g corn syrup

4 egg whites (at room temperature)

100 ml double cream

1 tablespoon lemon juice

2 tablespoons mint leaves (preferably 'chocolate' mint)

1 Peel ginger and cut into 2–3 mm dice, then bring to a boil with 500 ml cold water in a small saucepan over a moderate flame. Strain and repeat this process 3 times, using fresh water each time. Strain. Twist leaves from beetroot, then peel beet and cut into 4 mm thick slices and add to ginger with castor sugar and 500 ml cold water. Bring to a boil, then reduce to a simmer and cook for 2 hours until ginger is translucent and scarlet. Remove 2 tablespoons ginger 'jewels' while still warm and set aside (refrigerate remaining jewels in their syrup in an airtight jar for another time).

2 To make the ice-cream, cut the melon evenly in half lengthways. Place a small, fine-meshed strainer over a blender, then scrape seeds from melon into strainer, pushing seeds with the back of your spoon to release all juice. Discard seeds, then scoop melon flesh directly into blender. Ensure you end up with smooth, even shells, while avoiding the greening flesh towards the skin. Blend flesh to a smooth purée. Freeze melon shells in plastic bags.

3 Beat egg yolks and 90 g of the castor sugar until pale and thick. Warm corn syrup gently in a saucepan, add yolk mixture and whisk over a low flame for several minutes until thick and warm, then pour through a fine-meshed strainer into a large bowl along with melon purée.

4 Beat egg whites and 'rain' in remaining 1 tablespoon castor sugar until softly peaking, then fold with cream into melon mixture and add lemon juice. Churn mixture in an ice-cream machine according to the manufacturer's instructions. Tear mint leaves into small pieces and fold through ice-cream with ginger jewels. Fill frozen shells with ice-cream and smooth surface, then cover well with plastic film and freeze overnight or until set. To serve, cut each shell into 2–3 wedges with a sharp knife.

Passionfruit and Cardamom Ice-cream Swirl

Have some fun with this luscious ice-cream and sorbet combo!

SERVES **4–6**

1 teaspoon cardamom pods

650 ml pouring cream

125 ml milk

6 egg yolks

225 g castor sugar

2 oranges

6 passionfruit

1 ripe banana

1 Grind cardamom pods in a spice grinder or mortar and pestle and rub through a fine-meshed strainer into a small, heavy-based saucepan, discarding debris. Add cream and milk and bring to a boil over a moderate flame. Have on hand a fine-meshed strainer and a large bowl with a layer of ice-cubes in it to cool custard swiftly the moment it's cooked. Meanwhile, whisk egg yolks with 175 g of the castor sugar until pale, then pour in boiling cream. Whisk briefly, then return to pan over a low flame and cook, stirring constantly with a wooden spoon, until custard coats back of your spoon. It is imperative not to let the custard boil and scramble, yet it should congeal slightly at the base of the pan. Strain custard back into bowl and sit over ice to chill.

2 Meanwhile, juice oranges. Halve passionfruit with a small, serrated knife and scoop out pulp into a fine-meshed strainer set over a blender. Push pulp through strainer, then run seeds through a juice extractor and flush with orange juice. Add juice and peeled and chopped banana to blender and whiz for several minutes until smooth. In a small saucepan, heat about ½ cup of this purée with the remaining 50 g castor sugar, stirring with a wooden spoon over a moderate flame for a few seconds until sugar has dissolved. Return this to main purée and check sugar level. As some passionfruit are sharper than others, you may wish to dissolve in a little more sugar, although it is ideal to keep the mixture slightly sharp. Refrigerate until chilled.

3 Churn both cardamom custard and passionfruit purée, separately, according to the manufacturer's instructions, then set to swirl. Scoop spoonfuls of ice-cream and sorbet randomly into a large bowl. Fold together in several smooth motions, then tip into a lidded freezer container and firmly push out air with a sheet of plastic film pressed onto the surface. Return to freezer for several hours until just firm enough for serving.

Even grown-ups beam with child-like delight when served a scoop of colourful ice-cream swirled with vibrant ripples.

Champagne Ice-cream with Raspberry Ripple

For a number of reasons, this Champagne ice-cream recipe has stayed in my mind from my days preparing desserts at Berowra Waters Inn. There, Gay Bilson taught me the double-boiler technique used here as an ideal method for lightening (and cooking) the egg base for Bavarian creams. Implementing this aeration method with a Champagne ice-cream, rather than using the traditional process of cooking the custard directly over heat, not only seemed ingenious but also respectful to the bottle's fine bubble.

Nevertheless, I often wonder what the house of Bollinger would think of such adulteration, and am sympathetic to questioning of the need for such a premium brand. After all, who could really tell the difference between French Champagne and a cheap bottle of sparkling wine once it's immersed in eggs, sugar and cream? But if I am to honour the 'honest kitchen' ethic, I have to admit that 'sparkling wine' ice-cream, comparatively, just doesn't excite. Simple as that. So, what I've decided is that it all comes down to a sense of occasion, and to that end I've added a little more decadence with a ripple of raspberry!

For an extra-special event, think about taking this ice-cream to even giddier heights by making a meringue and ice-cream castle. Triple the quantities for the meringues on page 138 and make three baking trays worth of nicely peaked, tablespoon-sized meringues. Starting with concentric circles, and alternating blobs of ice-cream and meringues, build your castle on the chilled base of a springform tin. Aim for a sandcastle shape rather than the full turreted affair! Freeze the castle until firm (or up to 3 days), then present with a flourish.

SERVES 10–12

3 eggs
9 egg yolks
1 × 750 ml bottle Champagne
550 g castor sugar
1 litre pouring cream
6 × 250 g punnets raspberries
few drops of lemon juice

1   Choose a large pan that will hold a very large stainless-steel bowl snugly so that the water just touches its base. Bring this pan to a boil over a moderate flame. Put eggs, egg yolks, Champagne and 400 g of the castor sugar into the bowl and whisk continuously over the pot with a large balloon whisk for about 20 minutes until light and peaking. Remove from heat, then pour in cream and gently stir with a ladle. Refrigerate until chilled.

2   Push raspberries through a fine-meshed strainer into a jug and discard seeds. Gently heat about ½ cup of this purée in a small saucepan with remaining 150 g castor sugar, stirring constantly with a wooden spoon until sugar has dissolved. Mix in lemon juice, checking acidity (you may need a touch more sugar), then leave to cool.

3   Churn Champagne custard and raspberry purée, separately, according to the manufacturer's instructions, then set to swirling. Scoop spoonfuls of ice-cream and sorbet randomly into a large bowl. Fold together in several smooth motions, then tip into a lidded freezer container and firmly push out air with a sheet of plastic film pressed onto the surface. Return to freezer for several hours until just firm enough for serving.

Blood Oranges with Rhubarb Sorbet and Florentines

I must confess to Sybaritic fantasies aroused by the ambrosial, raspberry 'blood' of these exotic oranges. Heady with textures, this dessert titillates with its combination of juicy segmented fruit, spicy sorbet and delicately chewy florentine, made, ideally, with the candied peel of those fabulous oranges.

SERVES **4–6**

500 g rhubarb

150 g castor sugar

8 blood oranges

1 star anise

1 cinnamon stick

1 clove

4–6 Florentines (see page 156)

1   Trim leaves from rhubarb, then wash stalks well and cut into 2 cm lengths. Put the rhubarb into a heavy-based saucepan with the castor sugar and finely grated zest and juice of 2 of the oranges. Tie spices tightly in a small piece of muslin, then add to pan and bring to a boil over a moderate flame. Reduce to a simmer and cook for 10 minutes, stirring now and again to prevent catching, then leave to cool. Remove muslin bag and purée rhubarb in a blender. Churn in an ice-cream machine according to the manufacturer's instructions.

2   Segment remaining blood oranges by slicing off just enough from tops and bottoms to reveal inner flesh. Using a small sharp knife and cutting down orange, cut skin and pith away in strips. Holding orange over a small bowl, carefully cut segments free by sliding your knife down either side of connective tissue. When you're finished, give remnants a final squeeze into bowl before discarding.

3   Serve segments drizzled with juice, topped with a scoop of rhubarb sorbet and accompanied by a florentine.

Florentines

I've found the best florentines to be temperamental. Their texture tires with the merest breath of humidity and they deeply resent refrigeration, so it's best to make them in the cooler months when they can be stored happily at room temperature. This always seems to be when rhubarb and blood oranges are in season, making this spiced 'jaffa' trio a match made in heaven!

If you want to make just enough florentines to serve with the rhubarb sorbet on page 154, simply use a quarter of the quantities given here. But, then, why wouldn't you want to make a full batch of these chewy, chocolatey treats?

MAKES 16–20

120 g almonds
½ cup candied orange peel (see page 172)
120 g unsalted butter
80 g castor sugar
1 tablespoon flaked almonds
1 tablespoon currants
1 tablespoon pouring cream
150 g finest-quality dark chocolate

1   Preheat oven to 160°C and line 2 baking trays with baking paper. Chop whole almonds and candied peel separately into rough 2 mm pieces. In a small saucepan, melt butter over a low flame, then stir in castor sugar and slowly bring to a boil. Stir in chopped and flaked almonds, peel, currants and cream, then remove from heat. Spoon 2 cm blobs of mixture onto baking trays, leaving several centimetres between each, then bake for 9 minutes until evenly deep golden (you may need to bake the florentines in batches). Remove from oven and tidy up uneven edges with a metal spatula or fish slice while still hot, then leave to cool.

2   Gently melt chocolate in a double boiler, then stir briefly to even the gloss. Carefully turn biscuits over, then paint chocolate evenly onto each smooth base with a pastry brush. Leave to cool to room temperature before serving or storing in an airtight container.

The lively syrup from candying peel is great for enhancing ricotta or mascarpone...
←

Bees for Rent

I reckon Manoo's bee obsession is all thanks to the sign we once clocked on our drive to the shack offering 'Bees for rent'. Within months he was a registered apiarist, busying himself with the meticulous craft of hive-making before proudly branding each his own. There was no turning back . . .

Introducing the 'nucleus' was the next step. The whole mysterious process took weeks, from the time Manoo painted, stamped and dropped the hives off to the bee supplier to our undercover night-time pick-up, organised so the bees wouldn't catch on. We're talking live bees, hundreds of 'em, and a nail-biter of a drive around bends, up mountains, to get them. Despite our quarry being strapped into the back of the ute, Manoo spent the trip insisting I didn't stop suddenly. Then, of course, the spitting rain really started to piss down, and with a final veering around a corner into our orchard, a spin of the wheels bogged us – deep. Manoo got out to inspect – things were crook. The strapping had slipped, honey had oozed and the bees were going crazy! After several hair-raising slips in the mud, we somehow managed to land the buzzing boxes and bolt to the shack. Strangely, we didn't get stung.

That happened months later when Manoo got out his new outfit. Perhaps the bees found the 'space suit' offensive. Whatever caused their indignation, a floppy fold in the sleeve led to near disaster. He had made it clear to me on the first official visit to the hives that if one of us got stung we were to run to the shack and shut every door and window – apparently a single sting would alert the hive and cause a frenzy. So I did!

I left a sore Manoo to rob the hives with his 'taming' smoke-box and delicate brush. It only took ten or fifteen minutes before I was called back to help lug a heavy crate of frames. Now, I was told, the bees can't physically sting because their legs are too heavy with honey. I had to trust him . . .

I couldn't wait any longer. All that was needed was a hot knife to slide down the neatly waxed honeycomb capping to get to the heavenly nectar, then we scooped away like a couple of wild bears. I'm sure it was all the more ambrosial thanks to the length of our journey to this point – the wait an effective seduction I'm prone to employ on occasional guests, purely for the heightened enjoyment of all!

Manoo's other essential tool is the 'spinner'. Once both waxed sides are sliced off three frames, in they go. With a churn of the handle, the centrifugal force throws the honey all over the walls and down to the base of the drum. The smell is an absolute blast! A fine strainer set over a suitable jug is ideal to sit under the spout (to catch wax bits or the odd bee) before lifting the tap.

We had a friend visiting the day of our most recent rob who, we discovered, is highly allergic to bees. She was remarkably polite about it all considering the slightly 'Hitchcock' moment that overtook us in the shack as the bees grew increasingly curious about the smell of their honey baking with a few pears from the orchard . . .

Tropical Sorbets

Along with the heavenly, tropical, perfumed flavours of mango and coconut, the unique tang of a soursop is, for me, utterly unbeatable. If you haven't already indulged in this treat, the soursop is now grown commercially in Far North Queensland and is available in markets and Asian food stores elsewhere in the summer months.

As refreshing as each flavour is individually, I love to serve a scoop of all three sorbets, piled up together. It's hard to put a cap on how many these three recipes will serve – modestly six to eight, although it all depends on the covet of a favoured flavour, and obviously the size of your scoop!

Sister of the sweetsop (grown in cooler climates and affectionately known here as the custard apple) the exciting, velvety sherbet of the soursop makes the best summer cocktail or sorbet.

SOURSOP SORBET

2 perfectly ripe soursops

150 g castor sugar

LIME AND MANGO SORBET

4 limes

4 ripe, fragrant mangoes

200 g castor sugar

TOASTED COCONUT SORBET

1 brown coconut (husk removed)

1 litre milk

250 g castor sugar

½ teaspoon salt

1 vanilla bean

1   To make the soursop sorbet, cut each fruit in half, then lift out cream-coloured, V-shaped core and discard. Use your fingers to squeeze each seed free from fibrous membrane, then peel off skin. Double-check all seeds have been removed from hidden pockets before puréeing pulp in a food processor. Push pulp through a fine-meshed strainer to remove excess fibre. In a small saucepan, heat about ½ cup of this purée with the castor sugar, stirring with a wooden spoon over a moderate flame for a few minutes until sugar has dissolved. Return this to main purée and check sugar level – you may wish to dissolve in a little more sugar. Allow to cool. Churn in an ice-cream machine according to the manufacturer's instructions.

2   To make the lime and mango sorbet, squeeze juice from limes into a blender and add all pulp collected in the process too. Cut cheeks from each mango and scoop out flesh with a large spoon in one confident motion. Peel away skin surrounding each seed, then squeeze off remaining flesh. Add mango to blender and purée until smooth. In a small saucepan, heat about a third of this purée with the castor sugar, then follow remaining steps for soursop sorbet above.

3   To make the toasted coconut sorbet, preheat oven to 180°C. Hold coconut over a bowl to catch juice (you need to save this for later) and crack it in the centre with several short, sharp taps with back of a cleaver or a heavy knife. Check freshness by tasting juice and ensuring flesh is squeaky, firm and pure white, particularly where it meets the shell. Put coconut halves into oven for about 20 minutes until moisture has evaporated and flesh has shrunk slightly from shell. Wrap your hand in a cloth and remove coconut from oven, then, using a pair of tongs, slide one 'arm' between flesh and shell, pushing and twisting persuasively to free flesh. Break flesh into small pieces and whiz to a coarse paste in a food processor. Tip coconut paste onto a baking tray lined with baking paper and return to oven to toast for about 10 minutes until deep golden, stirring halfway through. Tip toasted coconut into a saucepan with saved coconut juice, milk, sugar and salt, then scrape in seeds from split vanilla bean and bring to a boil. Reduce to a simmer and cook for 30 minutes. Leave to cool before firmly pushing through a fine-meshed strainer. Refrigerate until chilled, then churn in an ice-cream machine according to the manufacturer's instructions.

Panna Cotta with Blueberry Compote

This recipe came into my kitchen via my dear friend Marie Zarro from Castellina in Chianti, Italy. The timing was impeccable; back then panna cotta had yet to become fashionable and my nostalgic yearning for Italy was satiated, albeit briefly, by the first heavenly mouthful.

Panna cotta is simple to make and you can vary infusions to suit – try orange zest, cloves or even a few rose petals. I tend to serve it surrounded by various colourful berry compotes, blueberries giving the liveliest burst in the mouth, especially when half the berries are left uncooked.

SERVES 6

3 leaves gelatine
1 litre pouring cream
150 g castor sugar
finely grated zest of 1 orange
1 vanilla bean

BLUEBERRY COMPOTE

1 orange
1 lemon
3 punnets blueberries
⅔ cup castor sugar
1 pinch salt
freshly ground black pepper

1 To make the panna cotta, soak gelatine leaves in plenty of cold water for several minutes to soften them, then squeeze out excess water. Put cream, castor sugar and orange zest into a small heavy-based saucepan, then scrape in seeds from split vanilla bean and bring to a boil. Add softened gelatine, stirring until dissolved, then strain into a jug and pour into 6 × 125 ml dariole moulds or a serving bowl. Cover with plastic film while still hot to prevent a skin forming and refrigerate overnight to set.

2 Finely grate zest of orange and lemon, then juice and strain. Put half the blueberries into a small saucepan with remaining ingredients, including several fine grinds of pepper, and bring to a boil over a moderate flame, stirring occasionally. Continue cooking until syrup coats back of a spoon. Skim any scum away and leave to cool to room temperature before adding rest of berries.

3 Turn out each panna cotta by simply pushing all the way around the rim of mould and with a sharp tap and a shake of the wrist the sexy blob will happily emerge. If you've set the panna cotta in a bowl, simply use a large spoon to scoop out and carefully invert the quivering panna cotta onto serving plates. Serve with blueberry compote at room temperature.

Chocolate Self-saucing Puddings

I can see how these chocolate 'self-saucing' puddings could torment the pedant, mainly because they don't, in fact, sauce themselves – you have a hand in it. Made without flour, they may also be accused of not really being puddings at all – merely cooked mousse, with sauce. Despite these afflictions, they remain a popular winter treat, served perhaps with a scoop of Chestnut and Honey Ice-cream (see overleaf) or even just a dollop of cream.

The puddings can be made well in advance and steamed for several minutes to reheat before serving.

SERVES **6**

200 ml pouring cream
325 g best-quality dark chocolate
3 large eggs (at room temperature)
75 g soft brown sugar
1 pinch ground cinnamon
1 pinch salt
50 g castor sugar
125 g double cream

1   Fill a small saucepan with water to several centimetres from the top and bring to a boil. Put pouring cream and 125 g of the chocolate into a double boiler. Turn off flame and leave chocolate to melt for several minutes before stirring to combine. Divide evenly between moulds.

2   Preheat oven to 200°C. Gently melt remaining chocolate in a double boiler, then stir briefly to even the gloss. Separate eggs and whisk yolks with brown sugar and cinnamon for several minutes until thick. Whisk egg whites with salt in a warm, clean and dry bowl until softly peaking, then gradually 'rain' in castor sugar, whisking to stiff peaks. Gently fold a little of the whites into the chocolate, then tip this back into the whites with yolk mixture and double cream and gently fold together. Divide mixture between 6 × 125 ml dariole moulds (or 8.5 cm wide × 6 cm deep ramekins). The mixture should ideally come no higher than 1 cm from the top.

3   Stand moulds in a large baking dish lined with a folded tea towel and fill with boiling water up to the pudding line, then carefully slide into oven. Reduce heat to 180°C and bake puddings for 40 minutes before serving turned out of their moulds with a dollop of cream or a scoop of ice-cream.

Roasted Chestnut and Honey Ice-cream

An ambrosial chestnut honey from Italy inspired this dish, but until someone here comes up with one, any honey will do. I like to serve a scoop of this ice-cream alongside our Chocolate Self-saucing Puddings (see previous page) or you can simply pour some dark chocolate sauce over the top.

SERVES **4–6**

125 g chestnuts

250 ml milk

600 ml pouring cream

1 large pinch salt

1 vanilla bean

6 egg yolks

125 ml honey

1   Preheat oven to 180°C. Using a small, sharp knife, make a little criss-cross incision at the fatter end of each chestnut. Bring a small saucepan of water to a boil, then blanch nuts for several minutes, removing the nuts one at a time into a clothed palm to peel, stripping away both outer tough and inner furry skins. This is much easier to achieve while the nuts are as hot as possible. Grind chestnuts to a coarse, sandy paste in a food processor or mortar and pestle, then spread evenly over a shallow baking tray. Toast in hot oven for 5–10 minutes, stirring occasionally, until deep golden.

2   Pour milk, cream and salt into a small saucepan, then scrape in seeds from split vanilla bean. Add toasted chestnuts and bring to a boil over a moderate flame. Reduce to a simmer and cook for 30 minutes, stirring occasionally.

3   Have on hand a fine-meshed strainer and a large bowl with a layer of ice-cubes in it to cool custard swiftly the moment it's cooked. Meanwhile, whisk egg yolks with honey to combine, then pour in hot milk infusion. Whisk briefly, then return to pan over a low flame and cook, stirring constantly with a wooden spoon, until custard coats back of your spoon. It is imperative not to let the custard boil and scramble, yet it should congeal slightly at the base of the pan. Strain custard back into bowl and sit over ice to chill. When cold, churn in an ice-cream machine according to the manufacturer's instructions.

Chocolate Mousse Cake

What I admire most about this modest cake is that she was originally a sunken flop that found fame thanks to a clever cook named John Stevenson and a rescuing upper coif of mousse. She is now extremely popular at social gatherings, often further embellished with a ruffle of the darkest chocolate.

230 g best-quality dark chocolate
230 g unsalted butter
8 eggs (at room temperature)
230 g castor sugar
1 pinch salt
finest Dutch cocoa (optional)
best-quality dark chocolate shavings (optional)

MOUSSE
175 g best-quality dark chocolate
5 eggs

1   Preheat oven to 180°C. Line a 30 cm springform tin with baking paper. To make the cake, melt chocolate and butter together in a double boiler over a gentle flame, stirring occasionally to combine. Meanwhile, separate eggs and beat yolks with half the castor sugar until thick and pale. In a separate large, warm, clean and dry bowl, whisk egg whites with salt until softly peaking, then gradually 'rain' in remaining sugar, whisking to stiff peaks. Fold chocolate mixture into yolks, then fold in whites to combine and pour into lined tin. Bake for 45–50 minutes until set. Remove from oven and leave to cool in tin. Don't worry about the cake sinking in the middle – it's meant to.

2   To make the mousse, gently melt chocolate in a double boiler, then stir briefly to even the gloss. Meanwhile, whisk eggs in an electric mixer for about 5 minutes until thick and pale. Fold both mixtures together and pour into sunken cake (still in its tin), then refrigerate for several hours until set. Decorate (if so inclined) with a dusting of the finest bitter cocoa and a few slightly softened chocolate 'ruffles' and serve with berries and perhaps cream.

Jenny's Baked Custard with Rhubarb

Jenny Learmonth was my vital right-hand, food-loving buddy for many years and perfected this recipe with my hankering in mind. For me, her baked custard is unsurpassed as the ephemeral grown-up version of the aluminium-tasting, powdered one served at boarding school.

To make individual custards rather than one large one, I like to bake the stewed rhubarb underneath rather than serving it separately. I also cut the rhubarb slightly smaller and reduce its syrup a little further to avoid any watering down of the velvety custard.

SERVES **6–8**

300 ml milk

450 ml pouring cream

1 vanilla bean

10 egg yolks (from 65 g eggs)

185 g castor sugar

1 whole nutmeg

RHUBARB

2 bunches deep-red rhubarb

295 g castor sugar

250 ml freshly squeezed orange juice

1 large pinch mixed spice

finely grated zest of 2 oranges

1 vanilla bean

1 Preheat oven to 140°C. Choose a baking dish that will hold 1.2 litres comfortably, ideally so the custard will sit just a few millimetres from the top.

2 To make the custard, put milk and cream into a saucepan and scrape in seeds from split vanilla bean, then bring to a boil over a moderate flame. Whisk egg yolks lightly with castor sugar, then whisk in vanilla infusion. Finely strain into baking dish and grate nutmeg liberally over the top. Line a larger baking dish with a folded tea towel, then stand custard dish on this and fill with boiling water to custard line. Carefully slide into oven and bake for about 40 minutes until set by checking with a very gentle wobble. Allow custard to cool completely in water before serving.

3 Meanwhile, trim rhubarb stalks of all green tops and wash thoroughly. Cut stalks into 2 cm lengths for individual custards, or up to 10 cm lengths if serving rhubarb alongside. Dissolve castor sugar in orange juice in a heavy-based baking dish large enough to take rhubarb in one layer. Add mixed spice, orange zest and rhubarb, then scrape in seeds from split vanilla bean and bring to a boil. Reduce to a simmer and cook rhubarb until just tender and still holding its shape, then remove with a slotted spoon. Reduce syrup to a saucing consistency over a moderate flame and pour over rhubarb. Serve warm, preferably.

Goat's Cheese Tart with Figs

With cheesecake in mind but wanting a little more flavour complexity, I came up with the idea of slightly sweetening goat's cheese and sexing it up with figs.

SERVES 12

1 heaped tablespoon sultanas

125 ml brandy or dessert wine

1 quantity Sweet Shortcrust Pastry (see page 199)

2 eggs (at room temperature)

200 g goat's cheese

2 tablespoons castor sugar

1 vanilla bean

1 pinch salt

200 ml double cream

finely grated zest of 1 orange

ripest figs

icing sugar (optional)

Fig and Vanilla Conserve (optional – see page 207)

1   Steep sultanas in brandy overnight (or longer). Make pastry, then line a 28 cm wide × 3 cm deep flan tin and bake blind (see page 199).

2   Reset oven to 180°C. Separate eggs. Put egg yolks, goat's cheese and 1 tablespoon of the castor sugar into a food processor and scrape in seeds from split vanilla bean, then pulse, scraping down the sides after a few seconds, until combined. Start whisking egg whites with salt in a warm, clean and dry bowl, then gradually 'rain' in remaining sugar, whisking to soft peaks. Gently fold in puréed cheese mixture, cream, drained sultanas and orange zest just until no streaks remain, then pour into prepared pastry shell. Bake for 40 minutes until golden, then allow tart to cool to room temperature. You may like to dust the tart with icing sugar and tear figs in half to sit alongside a serving, or you can arrange sliced figs decoratively on top and glaze them with some warmed jam.

Don't forget to select perfectly soft figs, bearing in mind that they only ripen on the tree.

Two Candied Peel Tarts

I love a buttery marmalade tart ('Duke of Cambridge tarding' to the English, according to M.F.K. Fisher) and have tweaked the filling over the years to sometimes include prunes, figs or candied ruby grapefruit tangled with slices of spiced quince.

Slices of candied peel are delicious dusted with castor sugar or with a coating of chocolate to serve with coffee. Save the syrup from candying to sweeten mascarpone or drizzle over pancakes.

SERVES **12–16**

1 quantity Sweet Shortcrust Pastry (see page 199)
500 g unsalted butter
6 egg yolks
250 g castor sugar *or* 250 ml quince poaching syrup

CANDIED PEEL

6 navel oranges *or* ruby grapefruit
castor sugar

QUINCE

3 ripe quinces
400 g castor sugar
750 ml dry white wine
1 star anise
finely grated zest and juice of 1 lemon
finely grated zest and juice of 1 orange
1 cinnamon stick
½ vanilla bean

1   Note that if making the ruby grapefruit and quince tart, the quinces need to be cooked overnight. Make pastry, then line a 32 cm wide × 3 cm deep flan tin. Bake blind and seal as instructed (see page 199).

2   To make the candied peel, quarter your chosen fruit (orange for the plain peel tart, grapefruit for the quince tart). Put fruit into a saucepan of cold water and bring to a boil, then drain and replace water and repeat process twice to remove bitterness. Weigh fruit and measure out same weight of castor sugar. Put fruit and castor sugar into a heavy-based saucepan and bring to a boil over a low flame, stirring frequently to dissolve sugar evenly. Reduce to a simmer and cook, stirring occasionally, for about 1 hour, until peel is evenly transparent. Remove fruit from syrup to cool on wire racks over trays.

3   Preheat oven to 140°C. To make the candied orange peel tart, melt butter over a low flame. Lightly beat egg yolks with castor sugar and slowly beat in butter until absorbed (don't overbeat). Scatter tart shell with thinly sliced candied orange peel. Pour egg mixture evenly over peel, then bake for 25 minutes until golden. Serve at room temperature.

4   To make the candied ruby grapefruit peel and quince tart, candy grapefruit peel as above. Peel quinces into acidulated water (saving skins) and cut fruit in half. Put remaining ingredients into a large ovenproof pan with 500 ml water, then press skins on top of syrup. Bring to a boil on stove, then transfer to oven with pilot light on and leave to poach overnight.

5   Next day, make the buttery custard as for the candied orange peel tart, replacing the castor sugar with 250 ml quince syrup. Scatter tart shell with thinly sliced quince and candied grapefruit peel before adding custard. Bake and serve as above.

Custard Tart Glazed with Finger Limes

Indigenous to Australia, finger limes are the caviar of the citrus family. The spiky trees prefer rainforest conditions, fruiting to the size and shape of a finger. Different plants may produce yellow, deep-purple, red or, most commonly, vibrant-green limes. But it is when you cut these limes in half that their true beauty is exposed – inside are tiny 'bubbles' of juicy flesh (the caviar!). Bursting with unique fragrance and tang, finger limes also bring an exciting textural 'pop' when squeezed over freshly shucked oysters or, as here, set in their own jelly over a custard tart, a lovely way to show them off.

For further crunch I like to use a handful of ground almonds when rolling the shortcrust pastry. Other times when making this dessert I substitute puff for the short pastry and make tiny, bite-sized, Portuguese-style tartlets.

SERVES **12–16**

1 quantity Sweet Shortcrust
   Pastry (see page 199)
800 ml pouring cream
300 g castor sugar
1 vanilla bean
4 eggs
3 egg yolks
1 Granny Smith apple
150 g Grade A finger limes

1   Make pastry, then line a 32 cm wide × 3 cm deep flan tin. Bake blind and seal as instructed (see page 199).

2   Preheat oven to 140°C. Put cream and 150 g of the castor sugar into a heavy-based saucepan and scrape in seeds from split vanilla bean, then bring to a boil over a moderate flame. Lightly whisk eggs and yolks together and lightly whisk in hot cream mixture. Pour mixture through a fine-meshed strainer set over a jug. Return tart shell to oven, pour in custard carefully and gently close door. Bake for 20–25 minutes until just set, giving the tin a slight wobble to check.

3   Make the glaze while the tart is baking (it needs to be applied while the tart is still warm). Roughly grate apple, skin and all, directly into a small saucepan, then use 500 ml water to wash excess from grater into pan. Cut each finger lime in half and gently squeeze and twist bubbles into a small bowl, picking out and adding any seeds and then all skins to the apple water. Bring apple pan to a boil, then reduce to a simmer and cook for about 30 minutes, occasionally prodding lime skins back under liquid. Pass through a fine-meshed strainer into a clean pan, pushing with back of a spoon to extract all juices, then return to stove with remaining castor sugar. Bring to a boil, stirring until sugar has dissolved, then boil rapidly to reduce by half. Remove and leave until cool to set like a jelly.

4   Using a spoon, break up jelly until smooth, then gently fold in saved lime bubbles. With a light hand, carefully smear surface of warm custard evenly with glaze and leave for around 30 minutes to set. This process can be hastened by chilling, although I prefer to serve the tart as is, at room temperature.

Finger limes are sold in the market by grade — choose Grade A limes, if you can, as these are larger and will save you time.

A Trifle Coming On

There's a summer party afoot and my contribution is the dessert. I can't resist the heady fragrance of the local peaches and, with their kernel in mind, I've also bought Ricciarelli, my favourite almond biscuits. I can feel a trifle coming on, but not the sort from my childhood that involved rainbow jelly layers, sliced banana and a blanket of coconut.

After a rummage for a pan perfectly wide and deep enough for a dozen peaches, I throw in a bottle of leftover white and a couple of handfuls of sugar. It's onto a full flame while I split a vanilla bean, scrape the seeds into a separate bowl and toss the pod in with the wine. I peel a 'snake' of lemon zest into the peach pan, then squeeze in the juice and top up the liquid with several cups of water and a bay-leaf. Meanwhile, I crack eight of the eggs we've collected, resting the yolks in the bowl with the vanilla, all ready for the custard. About two-thirds of a litre of milk is all we've got, so I put it on to boil with two little cartons of cream, saving a splash for later. Now the syrup's up to a rolling boil, so I gently plunge in each peach.

Back to my bowl with a generous handful of sugar, then it's a quick whisk of the yolks before I catch the swelling pan of cream. After a pour and a slight mix together, I'm back at the stove, taming the flame and swirling my wooden spoon hypnotically through the custard. I notice the peaches bobbing a little frantically, so adjust the heat with my other hand. At the next opportunity, I grab a fine strainer and sit it over the now-empty bowl. The motion is set; I stir and stir, with the odd roll of each peach when I can.

Surely a good 15 minutes has passed! My wrist is unstoppable, in rhythm with a tilting of the pan to check for the slightest curdle. At last I spot a relieving streak at the very bottom, then all's saved by the strainer and a swift splash of that leftover cream. Phew! Now I crumble in rough chunks of my biscuits so they can take up the cooling custard.

After a gentle squeeze, I lift each peach onto a large platter with a slotted spoon and can't resist a taste of their gorgeous pink syrup. A little extra sugar, a few more drops of lemon – oh! Now it's so gorgeous I have to blame it for a little sneaky diversion . . . I pour half the custard into a tray for the freezer and reach for a packet of gelatine leaves. Six will do, I reckon, so they're in for a cool-water soak before a stir through that spectacular syrup.

After a while the peach skins have wrinkled slightly and are cool enough to peel. In my element, I hold each peach over the syrup to catch every precious drop that bleeds as the skins slide free. I promise I'll fight every temptation to lick each one privately, then strain the nectar and slide in the naked fruit.

Finally I take a fork to the sides of the freezing custard, mixing it in well to break the icy crystals (a routine for which I'll need to stay sober, as there's no ice-cream machine here), then I get set to party!

The guests will get their delicious poached peaches with almond cakey-custard, oblivious to the fact that the following day their hosts (and perhaps any lucky stragglers) will be eating ice-cream and jelly!

Passionfruit, Mango and Coconut Tartlets

I feel no need to hyperbolise these tartlets. Hopefully, after all the initial preparation, you too will feel that the chosen flavours and textures speak for themselves.

MAKES **10**

1 quantity Sweet Shortcrust Pastry (see page 199)

10 passionfruit

1 lemon

1 Granny Smith apple

100 g castor sugar

5 large, ripe mangoes

COCONUT CUSTARD

1 brown coconut (husk removed)

1 litre milk

½ teaspoon salt

1 vanilla bean

6 egg yolks

½ cup plain flour

180 g castor sugar

100 ml pouring cream

1 Make pastry and line 10 × 10 cm tartlet tins, then bake blind as instructed on page 199. As these tartlets are filled with pastry cream, it is not necessary to seal the pastry.

2 Preheat oven to 180°C. To make the coconut custard, prepare the coconut by following instructions for removing, processing and toasting coconut on page 159. Tip toasted coconut into a saucepan with saved coconut juice, milk and salt, then scrape in seeds from split vanilla bean. Bring to a boil over a moderate flame, then reduce to a simmer and cook for about 20 minutes. Meanwhile, whisk egg yolks with flour and castor sugar for a few minutes to combine well. Push coconut infusion through a fine-meshed strainer directly into egg mixture and whisk well to combine. Tip back into pan and return to a boil over a moderate flame, beating continuously with a wooden spoon. Reduce to a simmer for around 15 minutes to cook out flour – don't panic about the formation of any lumps. Pour custard into a small bowl, then press plastic film onto surface to prevent a skin forming and leave to cool.

3 Scoop flesh from passionfruit into a small saucepan with finely grated zest, juice and seeds of lemon. Coarsely grate apple directly into pan, washing excess off grater into pan with 200 ml water. Bring to a boil, then reduce to a simmer and cook for 10 minutes. Push mixture through a fine-meshed strainer into a clean pan and return to a full flame with castor sugar. Check acidity – you may wish to add several drops of lemon juice at this point. Stir with a wooden spoon until sugar has dissolved, then boil steadily until reduced by two-thirds. Set aside to cool.

4 To serve, pulse coconut custard with cream in a food processor for a second or two until just smooth. Avoid over-puréeing as this will cause the custard to run (and, subsequently, the mango to sink). Cut cheeks from each mango and scoop out flesh with a large spoon in one confident motion. Peel away skin surrounding seed and thinly slice flesh (save seeds for a private snack or smoothie). Put a small, sneaky smear of custard under each tartlet before sitting them on plates. Spread in custard to half-fill tartlets. Express yourself with the arrangement of mango slices and delicately spoon over your passionate glaze.

Cœurs à la Crème

Since forming delicate cheese 'hearts' in traditional perforated porcelain moulds at Berowra Waters Inn in my early days, I now prefer to tie my 'cœurs' in natural ball shapes, which almost resemble real hearts, and save on accoutrements.

The recipe I make from memory these days includes whisked egg whites held with a further rebellious sprinkling of sugar. Some recipes use cottage cheese, mascarpone or even junket tablets, but fresh ricotta and crème fraîche make for delightful subtlety. I urge you to make your own 'cultured' cream. It is relatively simple and tastes better than many on the market.

I adore cherry compote made with a combination of cooked and fresh cherries. You can also serve your 'cœurs' in the traditional way with fresh raspberries or wild strawberries, if you can get them.

To make these little hearts, you will need a length of fresh, clean muslin.

MAKES **10**

800 g fresh ricotta

1 vanilla bean

3 egg whites (at room temperature)

1 pinch salt

100 g castor sugar

350 g Crème Fraîche
    (see page 198)

CHERRY COMPOTE

2 kg cherries

100 g castor sugar

finely grated zest and juice
    of 2 oranges

1 cinnamon stick

1 tablespoon kirsch

1   Rinse muslin well, then gently squeeze out excess water and cut muslin into 10 × 20 cm squares. Put ricotta into a food processor, then scrape in seeds from split vanilla bean and pulse for several seconds until just smooth. Scrape ricotta into a clean bowl. Whisk egg whites in a clean, warm and dry bowl with salt for several seconds before gradually 'raining' in sugar, continuing to whisk to firm peaks. Gently fold crème fraîche and whites into creamed ricotta until well incorporated. Lay muslin squares on workbench and divide mixture evenly between them. Bring corners of cloth together and tie tightly with twine. Hang cheeses in refrigerator by tying on a rack with a drip tray or cloth underneath and leave to set overnight.

2   To make the compote, wash cherries before removing stalks. Remove pips with a cherry pitter or by spreading cherries flat in a freezer bag and tapping persuasively with a mallet. Save half the best-looking cherries and put the other half into a small, heavy-based saucepan with castor sugar, orange zest and juice and cinnamon stick. Bring to a boil over a moderate flame, stirring until sugar has dissolved. Continue to boil gently for about 15 minutes until syrup reaches a saucing consistency and coats back of a spoon. Add kirsch, then remove from heat to cool.

3   Fold saved cherries through cooled compote and remove cinnamon. To serve, snip twine and upturn each little heart over its own pool of blood-red compote, then set free by carefully peeling away muslin.

Prune Truffles

These truffled prunes stuffed with almonds came to life through childhood memories of chocolate-coated raisins I'd sort from the nuts in our Christmas bowl as a kid. Now all grown up, even the seeds are edible!

The prunes can rest in the muscat syrup for weeks, if you like, leaving you free to whip up a batch of these at a moment's notice. (This syrup, by the way, is sensational over ice-cream or pancakes.)

MAKES 40

2 heaped teaspoons orange pekoe tea leaves

200 ml muscat

230 g castor sugar

40 pitted prunes

40 g blanched almonds

300 g best-quality dark chocolate

¼ cup finest Dutch cocoa

1   The day before you plan to serve these truffles, make an infusion of tea leaves in 200 ml boiling water. Add muscat and 2 tablespoons of the castor sugar, then strain over the prunes and leave to steep, covered, at room temperature overnight (or even for weeks).

2   Preheat oven to 180°C. Roast almonds on a baking tray for 8 minutes until deep golden. Meanwhile, line another baking tray with baking paper. Heat remaining castor sugar with 100 ml water in a small, heavy-based saucepan over a full flame, stirring until sugar has dissolved and syrup is boiling. Have a pastry brush and water on hand to clean crystals from sides of pan (if you don't, the crystals will end up in the syrup and set to a different texture, ruining your efforts). Continue to boil to a deep golden caramel. Remove from flame and gently throw in roasted almonds. Using a fork, ensure each almond is well coated with toffee, then swiftly scrape each nut on rim of pan on its way to the prepared tray to cool.

3   Gently melt chocolate in a double boiler, then stir briefly to even the gloss. Keep warm. Dip toffeed almonds, one by one, into chocolate, then remove with your fork, scraping in same manner as above, and return to tray. Refrigerate for about 10 minutes until set.

4   Using a fork, lift prunes from muscat syrup (save excess syrup for your next batch). Insert an almond where the plum's seed lived in a previous life. Dip each prune in remaining chocolate, rolling and draining as before, then return to tray and refrigerate until set. Roll prunes in cocoa to serve.

Forbidden Fruit

It's fruit-set time in the orchard and, despite delighting in the colourful sweep of rosellas and the teasing haw from the black cockatoos, life with the birds is a race to the finish.

To no avail we've dressed up the scarecrow, strung fake hawks from the most looming of heights, hung parties of old CDs spinning and flickering in the sun, and twisted various plastic snakes through branches that still seem to startle only us!

At first, the simple lying of nets over branches seemed ideal, despite the sad-looking appearance of the trees, but after months of growth bursting through the nets, it proves an impossible feat to cut them free without shredding leaves and damaging the next season's delicate growth.

Without rhyme or reason, tree by tree, we're outsmarted. The apricots, merely the size of cherry stones, have all vanished, yet the peaches are left to swell! The 'pleach', a hybridised plum–peach cross that I've snubbed since it was planted several years back by an insistent mate (I'm a bit old-fashioned and hopelessly romantic when it comes to heirlooms), is covered with motley, leather-skinned fruit – not a bird in sight. That'd be right.

But now it's late summer and the only fruit left in the orchard is that pathetic pleach, and curiosity's got the better of me. To touch, the leather's turned to velvet. With a gentle squeeze the fruit yields lovingly as it snaps from the branch. It's perfectly ripe! I bury each thumb as I prise the fruit apart, and a burst of scarlet 'blood' trickles around my hands . . . She's also a slipstone – and WHAT A BLUSH! Her snow-white heart bleeds a glistening scarlet, and the flavour – an ambrosial rush of raspberries! I'm left speechless, thrilled and giggling by the finest deception of all that's even outsmarted the birds.

I grab trays, and sheets of newspaper for padding, then pick away wildly as though some giant eagle might swoop in revenge. After several proud drop-offs, some of our now highly-prized pleaches have made it to the restaurant (under the guise of a 'raspberry peach') with poaching in mind, perhaps an almond-like ice-cream made with the leaves . . . Hmmm.

As thrilling as it was to slide the skin off our first raspberry peach, the poaching managed to morph all vibrancy from the flesh, leaving what scarily resembled a tinned plum! It just goes to show that some things are best left as Mother Nature intended.

White Chocolate and Rosemary Nougat

When making nougat it is imperative to use a sugar thermometer and keep a watchful eye. Honey, glucose, sugar and water are boiled to exacting degrees (thank you, Stephanie Alexander, for explaining this in *Stephanie's Feasts and Stories*) before being poured slowly into whisked egg whites – the rest is the fun part. Just remember to have everything on hand before you even think about dealing with the liquids.

Choose whatever dried fruit and nut combination takes your fancy. Prune and almond is a classic combination. Who knows, you may even warm to a 'tropical' cardamom, macadamia, candied ginger and saffron suggestion? This recipe uses pistachios and dried strawberries. The key to retaining the emerald green of the pistachios is to crisp them up slowly in a very low oven, and while you can buy dried strawberries from specialist food stores, the ambrosial aroma of your own strawberries drying is truly heaven s(c)ent!

MAKES **1.5 KG**

3 punnets fresh *or* 2 generous handfuls dried strawberries

150 g freshly shelled pistachios

200 g best-quality white chocolate

125 g unsalted butter

150 g candied peel (preferably orange or ruby grapefruit, see page 172)

4 large sprigs rosemary

4 sheets rice paper

440 g castor sugar

125 ml honey

250 ml liquid glucose

2 egg whites (at room temperature)

1 pinch salt

1 vanilla bean

1   If you are drying your own strawberries, start preparations at least the day before you want to make the nougat. Preheat oven to its lowest setting (even a mere pilot light, if using gas) or prepare a home dehydrator. Wash, hull and halve strawberries, then spread them out on baking trays lined with baking paper and dry in oven. Check them after 5 hours, then every 2 hours, to make sure they don't dry out too much and become crisp – they should still be pliable The strawberries will take 12–15 hours in a dehydrator. Remove dried strawberries and leave to cool, then store in an airtight container.

2   Preheat oven to 100°C. Roast pistachios on a baking tray for 1 hour. Cut chocolate into rough 1–2 cm chunks and chill in freezer. Cut butter into rough chunks and coarsely chop candied peel. Strip leaves from rosemary sprigs and chop finely (you should end up with about a handful).

3   Choose a 20 cm wide × 30 cm long × 4 cm deep baking tray. Line base with 2 sheets rice paper, folding it up the sides. Divide castor sugar, honey and glucose evenly between 2 heavy-based saucepans and add 30 ml water to each. Using a sugar thermometer, bring both syrups to a boil. Meanwhile, whisk egg whites with salt to soft peaks (preferably in an electric mixer). When first syrup reaches 125°C, drizzle it into whites while beating simultaneously. Bring other syrup to 157°C, then beat it into whites as well. Gradually whisk in butter to incorporate thoroughly. Fold in pistachios, dried strawberries, chocolate, candied peel, rosemary and seeds scraped in from split vanilla bean. Pour mixture into prepared tray, pressing remaining 2 sheets of rice paper firmly on top. Refrigerate overnight or at least for several hours until firm before cutting into bite-sized pieces.

There is nothing like being able to 'provide'. Everyone's larder, pantry or store cupboard is different, but any discerning home cook will always be able to offer up the makings of a meal, whether it's good canned tuna or tomatoes, dried pasta, chillies, spices, anchovies, capers, olive oil and the like.

A keen cook will also make the most of the seasons and squirrel away jewel-like preserves to be brought out when the fresh crop has finished. To be able to take down a jar of your own jam for breakfast (or to give away, if your supply is abundant and you can bear to part with it) has to be one of life's greatest pleasures. The same goes for the freezer: the satisfaction of knowing you have a growing bag of poultry bones for when you have time to whip up some stock, or enough stock to make a great soup, or a spare tart shell just waiting to be filled can't be described! And how to explain the joys of making a glossy, rich mayo with eggs from chooks you know ate yesterday's vegie scraps? Impossible.

Included here are my thoughts on a few basic ingredients I pull out of my own cupboards every day, and the recipes that I refer to over and over again.

Eggs

For those of us running our own hens, a 'fresh test' is invaluable, especially when it comes to wayward eggs. Simply fill a basin with water and put in the eggs one by one: a fresh egg will sink to the bottom on its side; if it rises slightly it is not perfectly fresh; if it floats, it is bad. When your eggs come in cartons, choose free-range, organic or biodynamic eggs, comforted by the thought that a Good Chook = Better Egg = Best for All!

Salt

I tend to use fine salt in cooking and salt flakes at the table. Fine salt is also best for sprinkling over anything fried (for example, the harbour prawns or blue-swimmer crabs on page 72) because fancier flakes of salt simply fall off. The decadent puritan can always grind these flakes down, but it's the texture of 'flake' salt that makes it so special in the first place. I'm especially fond of the gorgeous pink flakes of mineral salt from the Murray River (as opposed to imported sea salt) and like to think my enjoyment is helping desalinate the river too.

See also the recipe on page 196 for Gomasio, an addictive Japanese toasted sesame salt.

Olive Oil/Extra-Virgin Olive Oil

Plain, pure olive oil is ideal for general cooking or as the base to a mayonnaise, where other flavours are the essence and extra-virgin could dominate (see Asparagus with Pine-nut Mayonnaise, page 46).

General extra-virgin olive oils are great in salad dressings (see Goat's Cheese Salad with Golden Beets, Blood Orange and Radishes, page 55) and for the last-minute 'glossing' of stocks and pan juices, where the French would use butter or cream.

Show off a really special Australian first-press (new-season, unfiltered) extra-virgin olive oil by drizzling it generously over a bowl of soup or a piece of garlic-rubbed toast with a plate of double-peeled broad beans alongside, or use it as a dip for the freshest vegetables pulled straight from your garden. The main thing to bear in mind with first-press extra-virgin is shelf-life: because this oil contains more olive 'pulp' than other grades it tends to oxidise after a couple of months, so check the pressing date, buy sparingly and use liberally!

Parmesan

When a recipe calls for parmesan, I tend to use the Italian grana padano with pasta (see Linguine with Shredded Rocket, Lemon, Chilli Oil and Parmesan, page 23) or if it is included in something that is to be cooked (see Polenta with Braised Fennel and Olives, page 32). I save the finer, more expensive Parmigiano-Reggiano as a table cheese.

And a final word about buying organic

Just as a true macrobiotic eats food grown within a certain radius of where he lives, or a naturopath recommends honey from local flowers to heighten allergic resistance, there is a simple, natural logic behind eating organic food.

Choosing unadulterated, GM-free, organically grown, sustainable food whenever possible makes us feel plain good. The murkiness that's rife in our food chain is put to bed and our own peace of mind is restored.

We can take a hands-on approach in our own garden by feeding it with well-rotted compost (chook or cow poo rather than a dose of pelleted chemical nitrates) and learn as we go that the ladybirds will eat the aphids . . .

Back to the deceptive world of retail, I suggest getting your hands on a copy of *The True Food Guide* from the True Food Network (www.greenpeace.org.au/truefood). Not only does it make for riveting reading, but it will also help you make more informed decisions about genetic modification in the food you may be consuming obliviously. For the keen gardener seeking heirloom seeds, contact The Digger's Club in Victoria (03 5987 1877 or www.diggers.com.au) for their inspiring seasonal catalogues.

Vegetable Stock

With vegetarians in mind, this makes an ideal substitute in recipes that call for chook stock (for example, Spring Soup, page 36, Roasted Red Pepper Soup, page 42, and Polenta with Braised Fennel and Olives, page 32). I recommend grating the base vegetables (onion, carrot and celery) before caramelising the onion and then adding the other ingredients to help maximise the extraction of the natural sugars, which means more flavour.

MAKES **1.8** LITRES

2 large onions

100 ml olive oil

2 carrots

2 sticks celery

4 cloves garlic

1 large leek

2 large, burstingly ripe tomatoes

1 generous handful mushroom trimmings

1 generous handful fennel trimmings

1 bay leaf

1 generous handful thyme

1 generous handful parsley stalks

4 peppercorns

2 litres cold water

1   Peel and coarsely grate onions. Heat olive oil over a moderate flame in a heavy-based stockpot. Add onion and sauté for around 20 minutes, stirring regularly, until deeply caramelised.

2   Meanwhile, coarsely grate carrot and celery, and roughly crush garlic. Finely slice leek, then wash it well in a colander submersed in water to remove grit, and drain. Roughly chop tomatoes. Add all vegetables and aromatics to pot with water and bring to a boil, then reduce to a simmer and cook for about 3 hours. Push firmly through a fine-meshed strainer and leave to cool to room temperature before refrigerating or freezing.

Chook, Game, Veal or Beef Stock

I always use bones that are meaty and free from excess fat – ribs give the best flavour, and brisket is also good. Marrow bones, even with the marrow pushed out, offer merely bone and prove a waste of time. When it comes to poultry (game or otherwise), carcasses, wings and necks with heads all make good stock, although the cockscomb's a little fatty. Leftovers from a roast chook are better still – just remember to take that lemon out of the chook's bum! If you wish your stock to set like jelly (handy for travel), there is an astonishingly high quantity of natural gelatine in an ox tail or pig's head or trotter, ideal for 'potting' or making a terrine.

Over the years I have adopted a freshening-up routine with these slow stocks: I omit the vegetables usually added at the start and add them to a second (shorter) simmering later on to breathe a new vitality into the broth. This lifts the darker flavours, giving them a fresh edge. For a cleaner-tasting, light stock, the simple solution is to skip the roasting and deglazing steps by simmering the bones, raw, with the caramelised vegetables, aromatics and water. This delicate broth is an ideal way to show off a dumpling or filled pasta, and is perfect for Spring Soup on page 26.

MAKES 8 LITRES (2.5 LITRES REDUCED)

5 kg chook or game carcasses *or* meaty veal or beef bones

10 litres cold water

2 bay leaves

1 handful parsley stalks

10 peppercorns

3 large onions

3 sticks celery

3 large carrots

150 ml olive oil

4 large ripe tomatoes

1 head garlic

1 generous handful thyme

2 handfuls leek trimmings

1   Preheat oven to 180°C. Spread bones evenly in a large baking dish (you may need 2) and roast for 40–60 minutes until deeply caramelised, giving the dish a shake and turning bones halfway through to avoid any burning. Discard all fat from baking dish, then tip bones into a suitably large, heavy-based stockpot. Deglaze baking dish by standing it over a moderate flame and adding a couple of cups of the water. Use a wooden spoon to rub all the congealed blood from the bottom, then add to pot with remaining water, bay leaves, parsley stalks and peppercorns. Bring to a boil, then skim away any scum and reduce heat. Simmer for at least 6 hours or even overnight, with a simmer mat slipped underneath (or in a slow oven, where merely a pilot light will do).

2   When you are ready to proceed, skim away any scum, then carefully pour stock through a coarse strainer into a clean container. Rinse out stockpot. Peel and roughly chop onions. Strip and discard leaves from celery, then roughly chop celery and carrots. Pulse these vegetables in a food processor for several seconds to make a coarse paste. Heat rinsed-out pot over a moderate flame, then add oil. Sauté vegetable paste for several minutes, stirring regularly, until deep golden.

3   Roughly chop tomatoes and cut garlic head in half across cloves, then add both to pot with thyme and leek trimmings, then pour in strained stock. Bring to a boil, then skim away any scum and reduce heat. Simmer for 1½ hours.

4   Pour stock through a fine-meshed strainer (lined with muslin, if you like) into a large, clean pot. Ladle away as much fat as possible, then drape sheets of paper towel across the surface to remove the last traces. If using the stock as a base for soups or broths, allow to cool and refrigerate or freeze. If using the stock for sauces, boil rapidly until reduced by two-thirds, then allow to cool before refrigerating. Use within 2–3 days or freeze.

Fish Stock

One of my first and most valuable lessons in the kitchen was observing how a simmering stockpot could extract flavours slowly to achieve different depths of finish. For example, fish and shellfish stocks retain their subtleties when simmered for a mere half-hour or so, whereas a gutsy chook, game, veal or beef brew relies on being simmered for several lazy hours or even overnight.

When making fish stock, avoid oily fish such as trout, tuna, mackerel and so on, and opt instead for white-fleshed fish such as snapper, cod or barramundi. I thoroughly recommend adding a handful of shallot skins to help with clarification and to leave the broth with a magical deep-golden glow (I freeze any shallot peelings I'm not using just for this purpose).

Having fish stock on hand (or frozen as ice-cubes) means you can deglaze the pan swiftly after turning out your fish. With a few herbs, a light squeeze of lemon and a big slurp of the best olive oil, the 'bones' of your sauce can be swirled together.

MAKES **2.5** LITRES

2 large onions

2 sticks celery

1 bulb fennel

2 large carrots

6 unpeeled cloves garlic

1–2 kg fish bones, skin and trimmings

150 ml olive oil

3 litres cold water

2 large ripe tomatoes

1 handful thyme

1 bay leaf

1 handful parsley stalks

6 peppercorns

finely grated zest of 1 orange

1 handful shallot skins (optional)

1 Peel and roughly chop onions. Strip and discard leaves from celery and fennel, then roughly chop celery, fennel and carrots. Transfer these vegetables to a food processor and add unpeeled garlic cloves, then pulse for several seconds to make a coarse paste.

2 Snap fish bones by bending them persuasively, or use a pair of kitchen scissors to cut bones into several pieces – this helps extract flavour. Set bones aside. Heat a medium–large, heavy-based stockpot over a moderate flame and add oil. Sauté vegetable paste for several minutes, stirring regularly, until deep golden. Add fish bones and trimmings to pot with water. Roughly chop tomatoes and add to pot with herbs, peppercorns, orange zest and shallot skins, if using. Bring to a boil, then skim away any scum and reduce heat. Simmer for about 30 minutes, then ladle or gently pour stock through a fine-meshed strainer (lined with muslin, if you like) into a clean bowl.

3 As the delicate flavour of fish stock is particularly swift to tire, it is best to freeze any excess on the day, when cool; then it will keep for weeks.

Prawn Stock

This recipe makes a simple, light stock with clear, pure flavours. Bear in mind, though, that what appears to be a rather nude broth can always be enlivened by a fruitier blush from lots of chopped tomato, ideal as a base for other types of soup or a gutsy shellfish risotto.

MAKES **2.5** LITRES

2 large onions

2 sticks celery

1 bulb fennel

2 large carrots

6 unpeeled cloves garlic

150 ml olive oil

heads and shells from 1 kg green prawns

3 litres cold water

1 handful parsley stalks

1 handful thyme

1 bay leaf

6 peppercorns

finely grated zest of 1 orange

1 Peel and roughly chop onions. Strip and discard leaves from celery and fennel, then roughly chop celery, fennel and carrots. Transfer these vegetables to a food processor and add unpeeled garlic cloves, then pulse for several seconds to make a coarse paste.

2 Heat a medium–large, heavy-based stockpot over a moderate flame and add oil. Sauté vegetable paste for several minutes, stirring regularly, until deep golden. Add prawn heads and shells, crushing them with a wooden spoon to release all juices and the tasty 'mustard' trapped in the heads. Continue cooking for several minutes to caramelise, stirring to avoid overcolouring.

3 Add water, herbs, peppercorns and orange zest. Bring to a boil, then skim away any scum and reduce heat. Simmer for about 45 minutes, then ladle or gently pour stock through a fine-meshed strainer (lined with muslin, if you like) into a clean bowl.

4 As the vibrant flavour of prawn stock fades rapidly, it is best to freeze any excess on the day, when cool; then it will keep for weeks.

With Prawn Chowder (see page 64) in mind, I like to make a simple, light stock to retain the purest corn 'glow' and that honest, natural sweetness.

Fish Essence

This fish essence is used in Fish Stew for Two (see page 96) but can also be used in risotto or pasta marinara. This quantity of essence gives you a chance to stock up the freezer.

If you don't have the chilli oil on hand, just mix a minced bird's-eye chilli with a splash of olive oil instead.

MAKES **2** LITRES

1 large onion

1 large carrot

2 sticks celery

1 large bulb fennel

1 head garlic

100 ml olive oil

1 kg shellfish heads and shells

1 generous handful thyme sprigs

1 handful parsley stalks

1 handful basil leaves

1 tablespoon cumin seeds

1 teaspoon fennel seeds

2 litres Fish Stock (see page 192)

500 g burstingly ripe tomatoes

finely grated zest of 1 orange

50 ml Chilli Oil (see opposite)

1 pinch saffron threads

1   Peel and finely chop onion and carrot (or roughly chop and then briefly pulse in a food processor until fine). Trim celery and fennel and finely dice as well. Cut garlic head in half, across cloves. Heat olive oil in a large, heavy-based stockpot over a full flame. Add onion, carrot, celery, fennel and garlic and sauté for several minutes, stirring frequently, until deep golden and nicely caramelised. Add shellfish offcasts with the herbs and cumin and fennel seeds, crushing shellfish heads with a spoon to release any tasty trapped 'mustard' and juices. Let everything caramelise for several minutes, stirring occasionally to prevent catching at base.

2   Deglaze pot with stock, then add coarsely chopped tomatoes with zest, chilli oil and saffron. Bring to a boil, then skim away scum and reduce to a steady simmer and cook for 1 hour before passing through a fine sieve or finest blade of a Mouli. Leave to cool to room temperature before refrigerating or freezing.

Shellfish Oil

This is an ideal way to use leftover heads and shells from prawns, crabs, bugs, freshwater yabbies or marron, so start collecting and freezing your scraps now. With a crystal-clear, ruby blush and deep, sweet flavour, a drizzle of shellfish oil will greatly enhance a fish soup, shellfish salad or seafood pasta, and it keeps for months.

MAKES 850 ML

1 large onion

1 carrot

1 stick celery

1 bulb fennel

1 head garlic

500 g green prawn heads and shells

finely grated zest of 1 orange

1 bay leaf

3 large sprigs thyme

1 litre olive oil

Peel onion and cut into rough chunks along with carrot, celery and fennel. Whiz in a food processor with unpeeled garlic cloves and prawn heads to a coarse paste. (Alternatively, coarsely grate vegetables, cut garlic in half across cloves and leave prawn heads whole.) Put paste into a large, heavy-based stockpot, then add orange zest, bay leaf, thyme and olive oil and bring to a boil over a moderate flame. Reduce to a steady boil and cook for about 1½ hours, stirring occasionally, until all moisture has evaporated and ingredients are crisp (if using frozen shells this may take up to 3 hours). Remove pot from heat, then strain through a coarse-meshed strainer and leave to cool to room temperature for several hours. When cool, gently ladle oil through a fine-meshed strainer lined with muslin, leaving sediment at bottom, and store in warm, sterilised jars or bottles.

Chilli Oil

This chilli oil has a wonderfully nutty, almost sweet, gentle lift, thanks to scraping out the seeds and frying the chillies with garlic. Apart from being the integral element in a bowl of Linguine with Shredded Rocket, Lemon, Chilli and Parmesan (see page 23), this oil is great in a salad dressing and can always be beefed up with freshly chopped bird's-eye chillies for those of us needing a bigger kick.

MAKES 2 LITRES

1 kg long red chillies

2 litres olive oil

1 head garlic

Split chillies lengthways and scrape out seeds, being sure to wear protective gloves. Put chillies into a heavy-based stockpot with the olive oil and peeled and lightly crushed garlic cloves. Bring to a gentle boil over a moderate flame, then continue frying until all moisture has evaporated and chillies and garlic are deep golden. Using a slotted spoon, lift out chillies and garlic pulp and leave to cool. Using a food processor or blender, whiz cooled chillies and garlic pulp to a coarse paste with just enough oil to lubricate the motion. Stir purée into remaining oil and store in sterilised glass jars. Shake well before use.

Gomasio

According to Michel Abehsera, author of *Zen Macrobiotic Cooking*, 'gomasio is our table salt. It is our heartburn remedy . . . if there is heartburn! It is an indispensable companion in case of seasickness. But only yin people get seasick; if you are yang, you certainly don't need it.' I get seasick, so maybe that's why I like gomasio so much. Apart from using it in the Brown Rice and Vegetable Pie (see page 18), I find that a generous sprinkling of gomasio will greatly enhance a bowl of steamed rice, a piece of pan-fried chicken or fish, or a simple sauté of vegetables. It really is utterly addictive.

3 parts sesame seeds
5 parts coarse salt

Rinse sesame seeds in a fine-meshed strainer. Toast salt over a low flame in a small frying pan until crystalline and sparkling. Grind salt very quickly, ideally in a suribachi (Japanese ridged ceramic bowl with a wooden pestle) or otherwise a mortar and pestle, until powdered. Toast sesame seeds over a moderate flame in a small frying pan, stirring constantly, until evenly browned. Add to salt and grind together to a powder. Gomasio will keep for up to 1 week stored in an airtight jar or frozen for longer in a super-airtight container.

Mayonnaise

There is no comparison between the sensuality of hand-made mayonnaise and that of its distant relative from the supermarket. The knack of making your own opens the door to a whole new repertoire of dishes as simple and impressive as a classic 'eggs mayonnaise', where boiled egg halves nest on watercress and are masked with mayonnaise, an anchovy and a sprinkling of snipped chives.

For an added blast, let loose in a mortar and pestle with a handful of your favourite herb (basil, rocket or French tarragon are memorable), pounding with a little salt for grip, then continue with a swap of the pestle for a small whisk or fork to amalgamate with mayonnaise. Then dollop away!

MAKES **1** LITRE
6 egg yolks
1 tablespoon Dijon mustard
50 ml white-wine vinegar
1 teaspoon salt
juice of ½ lemon
800 ml olive oil
1 tablespoon boiling water (optional)

Whisk egg yolks, mustard, vinegar, salt and lemon juice in a ceramic bowl until blended. Whisk continuously while slowly drizzling in olive oil until all has been absorbed. Whisk in boiling water for a slightly looser consistency, if you like.

Tartare Sauce

While I serve this with Prawn Cutlets (see page 74), 'Potatoes Tartare' is a staple of mine at home. Simply put a few little new-season spuds on to boil (skins and all) while making the tartare in a bowl just large enough to fit the spuds. Slip the eggs in to boil on top of the spuds and when all is set to go, and eggs are peeled, roughly mash 'em all together!

2 eggs

salt

1 small red onion

1 clove garlic

1 handful capers

1 handful cornichons

1 cup flat-leaf parsley leaves

2 egg yolks

1 heaped teaspoon Dijon mustard

3 teaspoons white-wine vinegar

150 ml olive oil

25 ml extra-virgin olive oil

finely grated zest of 1 lemon

freshly ground black pepper

1   Bring eggs to a boil in just enough lightly salted cold water to cover. When boiling, set timer for 7 minutes. Cool eggs under running water, then peel and chop roughly. Peel and finely chop onion. Peel and mince garlic. If using tiny salted capers, rinse well and then drain. Capers in brine just need to be squeezed well. Coarsely chop capers, cornichons and parsley.

2   Whisk egg yolks, mustard, vinegar and ½ teaspoon salt in a ceramic bowl until blended. Whisk continuously while slowly drizzling in olive oil and extra-virgin olive oil until all has been absorbed. Mix lemon zest and all prepared ingredients through mayonnaise. Check seasoning.

Forget the mortar and pestle for tartare sauce — it's the chunky texture you want, so there's a bit of chopping to do, which is best done by hand. →

Aïoli

I serve aïoli with the fried harbour prawns or blue-swimmer crabs on page 72, and it is fantastic spread on sandwiches instead of butter!

MAKES 600 ML

4 cloves garlic

500 ml olive oil

1 tablespoon coarse salt

2 large egg yolks

juice of 1 lemon

Peel garlic. Put 125 ml of the olive oil and 2 cloves of the garlic in a small frying pan and gently fry over a low flame until garlic is golden. Remove pan from heat and leave to cool to room temperature. Lift garlic out of oil and grind to a paste in a mortar and pestle with remaining raw cloves and salt. Using a small whisk or fork, whisk in egg yolks and lemon juice, then slowly drizzle in oil from pan and remaining olive oil until incorporated.

Crème Fraîche

Culturing cream for crème fraîche is a bit like making yoghurt. Overnight, somewhere cosy, buttermilk melds with cream into one of the most refined luxuries one can have on hand in the fridge. A dainty dollop on potato cakes, smoked salmon, a little roe or fresh horseradish is surely fit for a king, and lashings poured over a deeply caramelised tarte tatin will really make you squeal!

While I sit my glass jar of brew on the shelf above my stove to snooze overnight, with a stockpot simmering below, you can use a yoghurt maker, a Thermos flask in a warm spot, or the bottom drawer of an Aga, if you happen to have one.

MAKES 1 LITRE

1 vanilla bean

300 ml buttermilk

700 ml pouring cream

Split vanilla bean, put it into a clean 1 litre glass jar and pour in buttermilk. Warm cream in a small saucepan to 70°C, using a thermometer that is evenly submerged and not touching bottom of pan. Pour hot cream into jar with buttermilk, then screw cap on tightly, shake vigorously for several seconds and leave at warm room temperature overnight. Next day, shake jar vigorously again before chilling for several hours. Crème fraîche will keep for about 10 days, refrigerated.

Sweet or Savoury Shortcrust Pastry

This pastry is best made by hand on a clean, smooth surface. It can be made in a food processor using a pulsing technique, but it is easily overworked and can become tough.

While I have included one trick for preventing shrinkage, try this one as well. Chill your tart shell with all excess pastry left overhanging, ensuring the pastry is well tucked into the inner edges and up the sides. When chilled, trim the pastry to leave an excess of about 1 cm standing upright, making sure the foil is upright too, then blind bake it. The moment the tart shell is out of the oven, run a small, serrated knife carefully around the edge to neaten it off. You end up with a real mess of crumbs that need a meticulous brushing out, but the bigger trimmings are great with a cup of tea!

For a savoury version, simply omit the sugar and add a larger pinch of salt. The instructions below are for making a 32 cm wide × 3 cm deep tart shell.

150 g unsalted butter
200 g plain flour
1 large pinch salt
100 g castor sugar
1 tablespoon cold water
egg white or jam

1 Remove butter from refrigerator 30 minutes before you start. Sift flour, salt and castor sugar onto your workbench. Using a cheese grater, coarsely grate butter onto flour and rub through between palms of your hands until 'sandy' in texture. Drizzle on cold water, then squeeze gently until massed together. Form into a flat disc about 2 cm thick, then wrap in plastic film and refrigerate for about 1 hour.

2 Dust your workbench lightly with flour, then roll pastry to a rough 2–3 mm thick round (large enough to cover tart shell). Using a large knife, ensure pastry is free from bench and carefully roll it closely around rolling pin back onto itself, dusting off excess flour with a pastry brush as you go.

3 Lower pastry into a 32 cm wide × 3 cm deep flan tin and press well into edge. Run rolling pin over top of tin to cut pastry evenly. Press sides of tart gently to push pastry a couple of millimetres above rim. This allows for slight shrinkage when baking. Don't brush out flour from inside tart shell. Refrigerate shell on a baking tray for at least 30 minutes.

4 Meanwhile, preheat oven to 200°C. After brushing out excess flour from inside tart, stab pastry with a fork in several spots to avoid bubbling. To blind bake your tart shell, line it with aluminium foil and fill it with dried beans, rice or professional pastry weights, ensuring you fill adequately up sides (again to prevent shrinkage). Bake for 25 minutes until golden, then remove weights after checking pastry is set down sides to base. The pastry will be paler and need to be baked for a further 7–10 minutes without weights or foil to colour up evenly. When golden, seal shell with lightly beaten egg white or similarly coloured marmalade or jam (I like to purée my favourite Heavenly jam for this – see page 207 – and then paint it over evenly, ensuring fork holes are filled). Either way, return tart shell to oven to set for several minutes, then remove it from tin and carefully sit it on a wire rack to cool before filling as desired.

Ginger Beer

This little gem of a recipe came via a paperback I had knocking around for years, from memory claiming to be 'Australia's Own'. I kick myself for the loss, although raise a glass every time I partake to my imaginary 'Pop' and the nostalgic stories about his home-brew exploding in his backyard shed.

Due to the volatile nature of the slowly fermenting sugar, I suggest storing the bottles lying flat, refrigerated, inside a large plastic tub with a tight-fitting lid, just in case. And keep a tab on the date. After the first three days, the zesty, fine bubbles make the perfect digestive tonic. But past the first week, this fizz is best kept from the kids – one glass and the ginger will provide a lift right to the tips of your ears. Cheers!

MAKES 16 × 750 ML BOTTLES

3 lemons
12.5 litres water
300 g fresh ginger
1.75 kg castor sugar
5 level tablespoons cream of tartar
1 tablespoon dried yeast

1   Peel lemons, then finely chop peel. Juice lemons and keep for next day. Bring water to a boil in a very large stainless-steel stockpot, then remove from heat. Peel and grate ginger and add to pot with lemon peel, castor sugar and cream of tartar. Allow to cool to blood temperature. Cream yeast with a little of this liquid, then stir back into stockpot. Allow to stand for 12 hours.

2   Next day, strain, then add lemon juice and pour into sterilised bottles fitted with screw tops. Taste after 3 days and cellar for longer, if you dare!

Tomato Chutney

Like any favoured chutney, this one always goes down a treat when spread on Aussie toad-in-the-hole-style eggs, a steak sandwich or slices of the Christmas ham. It's hard to resist in an old-fashioned seafood cocktail, too (see page 76).

MAKES 1.5 LITRES

1 teaspoon fennel seeds
1 teaspoon cumin seeds
1 teaspoon brown mustard seeds
3.5 kg burstingly ripe tomatoes
8 red onions
4 cloves garlic
2 bird's-eye chillies
150 ml olive oil
300 ml red-wine vinegar
500 g soft brown sugar
1 generous handful thyme sprigs
200 g currants
salt
freshly ground black pepper

1   Toast fennel, cumin and mustard seeds together in a small frying pan over a low flame until aromatic. Blanch, peel and roughly chop tomatoes. Peel and roughly chop onions. Peel and mince garlic. Finely chop chillies.

2   Heat olive oil in a large, heavy-based pan and add onion, then cook until a deep caramel, stirring frequently. Add garlic and chilli and sauté for a few moments longer before adding tomato, toasted seeds, vinegar, sugar and thyme – stalks and all. Reduce flame to a simmer and cook until all excess moisture has evaporated (around 1½ hours), stirring frequently to avoid catching. Add currants and cook for a few final minutes, then remove the now-bare thyme stalks. Taste and adjust seasoning, then seal in warm, sterilised jars.

Red Pepper Chutney

This sweet and smoky chutney is perfect to serve alongside a sharp goat's cheese that has been dipped in breadcrumbs and then baked, and it cheers up a humble, wholesome lentil patty (see page 16).

MAKES 1 LITRE

8 large red peppers

100 ml olive oil

6 red onions

3 cloves garlic

½ teaspoon cumin seeds

½ teaspoon ground allspice

½ teaspoon mild Spanish paprika

1 generous handful oregano leaves

1 bay leaf

200 ml red-wine vinegar

125 g castor sugar

100 g sultanas

salt

freshly ground black pepper

1   Preheat oven to 200°C. Put peppers into a large baking tray(s) to form a single layer and rub half the olive oil evenly all over. Roast for around 25 minutes, turning at several intervals, until skin has puffed and slightly darkened all over. Remove from oven and leave to cool in tray to room temperature.

2   Meanwhile, peel and roughly dice onions and garlic. In a small dry frying pan, toast cumin seeds over a low flame until fragrant, then cool and grind.

3   Peel peppers by sliding off skins, discarding seeds as you go, then put them into a strainer over a bowl to catch all juices. Use a rubber spatula to scrape all roasted juices from tray(s) into bowl, then roughly chop peppers.

4   Heat remaining olive oil over a moderate flame in a large, heavy-based pan. Add onion and garlic and sauté for 5–10 minutes until deep golden. Add spices, herbs, vinegar, sugar and collected juices, then stir frequently until boiling. Reduce to a simmer and cook for about 1½ hours until excess moisture has evaporated, stirring regularly as needed. Add sultanas and return to a final boil before seasoning to taste. Remove from heat and discard bay leaf. Pour while warm into warm, sterilised jars.

Tins, Jars 'n' Packets

Apart from reminding me it's time for a deli run, our favourite 'pasta-della-cupboard' saves the day. I've my staple tin of tuna, half-filled jar of capers, lucky-last can of chopped tomatoes and several scrunched up packets of leftover pasta – a few shells, spirals and tubes. I fill up the pasta pot and head for the garden, making a beeline for the last flowering onions in a desperate quest to freshen things up. Like a ravenous rabbit I tear away at the parsley, then twist off a lemon on my way back in . . .

It's off with those onion roots before I peel and roughly dice the bulbs, pushing the pile to the side of my board. After a quick rinse and a few shakes of the parsley, I shred away at the leaves for a bit, then grate lemon zest over the top, leaving just enough room on the board to crush a couple of cloves of garlic.

With my pot rolling up to a boil, I throw in a three-fingered pinch of salt and clock the different cooking times on each of my pasta packets – I love the challenge of the high-wire juggle! A quick calculation later and I shake in the tubes, chased by my slotted spoon as it rows around the pot.

I peel back the lids from my tins and open the jar, pressing away the excess oil from the tuna and squeezing every last drop of brine from the capers. Just as I reckon the tubes' headstart to be up, I empty the spirals into the bubbling pot.

My frying pan's next to hit the stove, then in goes a slurp of olive oil. Within seconds the oil's warm to my palm, so I scatter in the capers, swirling them gently as they hiss at me and burst wide open. In my hypnosis I remember the packet of shells, my tight schedule hopefully now on course as they tumble in with their mates. My capers have darkened and crisped now, so I scrape in the garlic, letting it 'glow' for a second. Next those onions – a rough stir, then I leave them to JUST catch. I sprinkle in salt flakes, grind madly with the pepper and then blitz the parsley and zest by persuasively tossing the pan.

In no time I'm fishing away for my various bits, testing, testing and testing, to discover there's barely a minute to spare! Swiftly I flake in the tuna, slurp in some tomatoes, douse away with a bottle of chilli oil and trickle in a few drops of balsamic. I grab the plates, sit them at the bottom of the sink, set the colander on top and then tip in the boiling pasta, blowing instinctively at the steam to save my hands. After a quick flick of the wrist and a jump of the bits, I pour the lot back into the pot with the slightest trail of starchy water before stirring it all together and draining each scalding plate – OUCH – with my tongs!

Preserving

I naively opened the door to preserving when I opened our restaurant door for breakfast, comforted by the thought that any over-ripe fruit could be economically boiled into jam. Despite most attempts falling flat, they were a comforting reassurance to all in the kitchen (I hoped) that nothing need be wasted. The trouble was, we were in the public eye and charging good money. So, we got a little serious and with persistence and inspiration from a book or two on the subject, shelves went up and colourful jars began to fly out the door.

Whether making jam, its luxurious relative conserve or a citrus-based marmalade, the best results are achieved when using early-season, just-ripe fruit. Natural pectin levels are higher, cooking time is shortened and the preserve sets with glowing vibrancy truest to the colour of the fruit.

Use a wide, heavy-based pan and ensure there is plenty of depth to contain fiercely boiling quantities. Serious handforged copper preserving pans are a real luxury – the copper provides a swifter boil (from higher heat conduction) and so a superior result. Even an old washhouse 'copper' (sworn by many preserve enthusiasts as the secret to their show-quality results) can be used successfully.

I always try to remember the following pointers.

Simmer slowly to extract maximum natural pectin and gently soften any skins. Stir as needed to avoid catching and top up with a little water if the fruit becomes dry before it is tender.

Boil rapidly once the sugar has dissolved, to reach setting point as quickly as possible.

Wrinkle test by placing a teaspoonful of preserve on a small saucer in the fridge for several minutes to cool. Run a finger through the blob to see if the surface wrinkles. If so, the preserve is ready; if sloppy, return the pan to a swift boil and repeat this process in a few minutes.

Rest the pan (jellies excluded), with the preserve in it, for around 10 minutes until the preserve is just setting around the edges and still fairly hot. This prevents that floating look, achieving a more even distribution of fruit through the jar.

And the rest is a can of worms!

Apricot Jam

I reckon a little salt, vanilla beans and a few cracked kernels from the pips (toxic in large quantities) bring a lush sophistication to good old apricot jam.

MAKES **3** LITRES

2.5 kg just-ripe apricots

juice of 3 lemons

½ teaspoon salt

2 vanilla beans

1.5 kg castor sugar

1   Wash and cut apricots in half, saving 6 pips. Crack pips with a metal mallet or hammer and remove kernels, ensuring each kernel is lightly crushed to release its nutty flavour. Pour lemon juice into a preserving pan with apricots and salt, then SIMMER SLOWLY, stirring frequently, for about 20 minutes.

2   Split vanilla beans lengthways, then cut each into 3 pieces and add to pan. Stir in sugar until dissolved, then BOIL RAPIDLY until setting point is reached. WRINKLE TEST after 10 minutes, then more frequently until set. Add cracked kernels to pot at setting point so they don't boil to mush. REST THE PAN for about 20 minutes for even fruit distribution, then stir preserve before storing in warm, sterilised jars, ensuring each jar gets its own piece of vanilla bean.

Banana Marmalade

The first time I tried banana marmalade I was intrigued by its gorgeous pink blush, naturally enhanced by acid from lemons or oranges. I am now hooked, and prone to further spicing from a few cloves, cinnamon sticks or star anise. I wonder what ginger would be like with it?

MAKES **3.5** LITRES

900 g lemons

2.7 litres water

2 star anise, cloves *or* cinnamon sticks

12 firm, not-too-ripe bananas

2.7 kg castor sugar

1   Cut lemons in half, then squeeze juice and set aside. Scoop pith from lemons with all seeds into a small square of muslin. Tie tightly and put into a large preserving pan. Finely dice lemon peel, then add to pan with water and chosen spice. SIMMER SLOWLY for 40–60 minutes, covered, until peel is tender.

2   Meanwhile, peel and dice bananas into rough 1 cm chunks and add to pan when peel is tender. Return to a boil, then pour in sugar, stirring until dissolved. BOIL RAPIDLY, then add lemon juice and continue boiling until setting point is reached. WRINKLE TEST after about 10 minutes, then more frequently until set. REST THE PAN for about 20 minutes for even fruit distribution, then stir preserve before storing in warm, sterilised jars, having removed spices, if you wish.

Fig and Vanilla Conserve

Use tiny, whole, perfectly ripe figs for this lush, seductive conserve (if your figs are large, just cut them in half). An initial slow steep helps to leach the fruit of water, therefore shortening the cooking time and 'conserving' the shape of the figs. This jam makes a great contrast if used to glaze the figs decorating the goat's cheese tart on page 170.

MAKES **1** LITRE

1 kg soft figs

1 vanilla bean

finely grated zest and juice of 1 lemon

1 kg castor sugar

1   Trim hard twigs from ends of figs. Halve or quarter figs if large, but leave whole if small, and put into a bowl. Scrape seeds from split vanilla bean into figs, then add bean halves with zest and juice of lemon. Pour in castor sugar and roll all together. Leave to steep for about 2 hours, covered, at room temperature.

2   Transfer steeped figs with contents of bowl to preserving pan. SIMMER SLOWLY for several minutes to ensure all sugar has dissolved, then BOIL RAPIDLY until setting point is reached. WRINKLE TEST after about 10 minutes. REST THE PAN for about 10 minutes for even fruit distribution, then stir preserve before storing in warm, sterilised jars with half a vanilla bean in each one.

Heavenly

'Heavenly' is the name given to this fantastic crossover jam/marmalade by the Country Women's Association of Tasmania. It's the real 'tutti-frutti', with perfect pectin levels every time!

MAKES **4** LITRES

2 oranges

4 lemons

500 ml water

6 perfect just-ripe peaches

6 perfect just-ripe Packham pears

6 Granny Smith apples

castor sugar

1   Juice oranges and 1 of the lemons and save. Finely chop the squeezed lemon, then SIMMER SLOWLY in a preserving pan with water until tender.

2   Meanwhile, cut peaches into 1 cm chunks, leaving skin on. Peel, core and cut pears into roughly same size. Put into a bowl with peaches and pour over saved citrus juice. Peel apples and grate into same bowl, mixing juice constantly through to avoid browning. Weigh all fruit together and return to pan to simmer while weighing an equal quantity of castor sugar. Add sugar to pan with the juice of the 3 remaining lemons, stirring until dissolved. BOIL RAPIDLY until setting point is reached, stirring occasionally to avoid catching. This may take about 30 minutes – use WRINKLE TEST. Finally, REST THE PAN for 20 minutes for even fruit distribution, then stir preserve before storing in warm, sterilised jars.

Mandarin Marmalade

For fruit with the highest pectin levels, choose the freshest, first-of-season mandarins, ideally picked straight off the tree.

MAKES 2 LITRES
1 kg mandarins
2 litres water
1 teaspoon salt
4 lemons
1.5 kg castor sugar

1   Cut mandarins in half, then squeeze out juice and pour through muslin to catch pulp and seeds. Scrape excess membrane into muslin as well, then tie muslin tightly together. Refrigerate strained juice. Put muslin bag into a large, clean bucket, bowl or jar with water. Cut mandarin peel into long ('julienne') strips or, alternatively, small dice, then add to water and leave to steep pectin overnight.

2   Next day, pour juice and water with peel into a preserving pan over a moderate flame. SIMMER SLOWLY with salt for 40–60 minutes, covered, until peel is tender.

3   Juice and strain lemons. Add sugar to pan, then BOIL RAPIDLY. Add lemon juice and continue boiling until setting point is reached. WRINKLE TEST after 10 minutes. REST THE PAN for about an hour until just setting around edges for even fruit distribution, then stir preserve before storing in warm, sterilised jars.

Mango Passion

With the tropics in mind, this glowing mango/passionfruit combo could also include the heat from a little chopped ginger, if you are so inclined.

MAKES 3 LITRES
10 lemons
4 Granny Smith apples
1 litre water
2.5 kg ripe mangoes (about 5 large)
20 passionfruit
2 kg castor sugar

1   Cut 2 of the lemons in half, then squeeze out juice and cut flesh and peel into 2 mm dice. Squeeze remaining lemons (freeze shells for another day) and top up lemon juice to make 450 ml. Coarsely grate apples, skin, seeds and all, into a large square of muslin. Add chopped lemon to apple with any seeds and tie muslin tightly together. Put muslin bag into a preserving pan with water. SIMMER SLOWLY, covered, for about 30 minutes, occasionally prodding muslin.

2   Meanwhile, cut cheeks from mangoes, then scoop out flesh with a large spoon in one confident motion and cut into rough 1 cm chunks. Peel away skin surrounding each seed, then squeeze off remaining flesh. Halve passionfruit, then scoop out pulp and push through a fine-meshed strainer. Save 1 teaspoon of seeds and discard rest.

3   Remove muslin bag from preserving pan, squeezing well, then add mango , passionfruit and lemon juice. When heated through, add sugar, stirring until dissolved. BOIL RAPIDLY until setting point is reached. WRINKLE TEST after about 10 minutes. Stir in saved passionfruit seeds. REST THE PAN for about 30 minutes for even fruit distribution, then stir preserve before storing in warm, sterilised jars.

Spiced Grape Jam

Due to the surprisingly low level of pectin found in most grapes, my grape jam usually ends up with the consistency of honey. In the hope of further natural pectin extraction, one can use grapes with seeds (removed and then wrapped in muslin) for barely noticeable results (hardly worth the effort) or add commercial pectin for a sure set – something I avoid in my (perhaps puritanical) jam-making pursuits. Of course, it's entirely up to you.

Even though requests for this 'jam' often can't be met because of its popularity, I am sharing its recipe mainly because I want to encourage a little improvisation with a potentially disappointing batch. Turn to Apple Fritters with Spiced Grape Ice-cream on page 146 to see what I mean.

MAKES **1** LITRE

1.2 kg seedless green grapes (preferably thick-skinned
   early-season grapes)
100 ml water
1 tablespoon mixed spice
finely grated zest and juice of 1 lemon
1.2 kg castor sugar

1 Pick grapes off stalks and wash well. Put grapes into a preserving pan with water, mixed spice and lemon zest and juice. SIMMER SLOWLY, stirring frequently, for about 10 minutes.

2 Add castor sugar, stirring constantly until dissolved, then BOIL RAPIDLY until setting point (or thick honey-like consistency) is reached – WRINKLE TEST after about 10 minutes.

3 REST THE PAN for about 20 minutes for even fruit distribution, then stir preserve before storing in warm, sterilised jars.

Acknowledgements

For a cook under pressure to let loose with a few simple recipes is a treat, and being given that opportunity by the most astute and exciting of publishers, Julie Gibbs, is, to say the least, a thrill beyond! Thank you, Jewels, for opening that door and for introducing my heady ramblings to the finest team in the business.

I am forever indebted to my editor, Caroline Pizzey, for her enthusiasm, and am in awe to have had my homework in her hands. The finest eyes behind the lens, photographer Simon Griffiths loomed and retreated with the deftest sensitivity. Stylist Carlu Seaver and her irresistible treasures added a magical touch to my food. It has never looked this good! Debra Billson constantly refined, then snuggled me into her considered design, overseen along the way by the capable Alison Cowan at the helm of the project. You have all made this journey an absolute pleasure.

To the cooks who have hired or inspired me (in alphabetical order) – Stephanie Alexander, David Allouche, Tony Barlow, Maggie Beer, Gay Bilson, Martin Boetz, Jacob Brown, Dany Chouet, Leif Etournaud, Lorraine Godsmark, Rose Gray, David Herbert, Prue Hill, Simon Hopkinson, Kylie Kwong, Janni Kyritsis, Christine Manfield, Franca Manfredi, Stefano Manfredi, Paul Merrony, Hans Mohr, Jamie Oliver, Anders Ousback, Tim Pak Poy, Gerard Pasquet, Armando Percuoco, Neil Perry, Damien Pignolet, Marianne Piotrowsky, Ruth Rogers, Phillip Searle, Virginia Wong See, George Sinclair, Rick Stein, John Stevenson, Martin Teplitzky, David Thompson, Hugh Wennerbom, and Marie Zarro – thank you for leaving indelible imprints and stirring my pot.

As the success of any restaurant lies largely in the hands of the sharpest suppliers, I wish to share mine and, in doing so, I thank them for the consistency and quality of their produce: Australia on a Plate (02 9667 1677), Chef's Warehouse (02 9211 4555), Craig Cummins Seafoods (02 9564 1727), The Digger's Club (03 5987 1877), Fratelli Fresh (1300 552 119), Joto Fresh Fish (02 9557 0533), La Dolce Vita Fine Foods (02 9587 4818), Nicholas Foods (02 9316 5656), Spiceland (02 9746 2996), Waverley Wholesale (0414 483 943) and Wrights the Butchers (02 9313 5228).

To every valuable member of our team at Sean's Panaroma, kitchen and floor, past and present: thank you. A special mention to Jenny Learmonth, Lisa Rutherford, Jacqueline Bourke and Alex Kearns.

My gratitude to Oliver Moran for helping me graduate from pen and paper scrawlings to the world of technical efficiency, to Mary-Ellen Hudson for making our clandestine existence a delight to legitimise, to Nellie and Hughie Benjamin for making our dream a reality, and to my Dad, Edmund John, who taught me how to be a self-made man.

I owe my deepest gratitude to Manoo for his patience and utter devotion. You are my rock!

Stockists

Many thanks to the following for supplying such beautiful props for the photography.

Accoutrement, (02) 9969 1031; www.accoutrement.com.au
Bed Bath N' Table, (02) 9960 3366, (03) 9387 3322
Bison, (02) 6257 7255; www.bisonhome.com
Camargue, (02) 9960 6234; www.camargue.com.au
Country Road Home, 1800 801 911; www.countryroad.com.au
Design Mode International, (02) 9998 8200
Honey Bee Homewares, (02) 9948 9908
Living with a Twist, (02) 9908 2700
Major & Tom, (02) 9557 8380
Mud Australia, (02) 9300 8377; www.mudaustralia.com
Papaya, (02) 9386 9980; www.papaya.com.au
Rapee, (02) 9496 4511; www.rapee.com.au
Rhubarb, (03) 9681 9922; www.rhubarb.net.au
Riedel Glassware, 1300 780 124; info@ambient.com.au
Rokoco, (02) 9818 2331; www.rokoco.com.au
Simon Johnson, 1800 655 522; www.simonjohnson.com
Wheel&Barrow, (02) 9938 4555; www.wheelandbarrow.com.au
Your Display Gallery, (02) 9906 7556

Bibliography

Abehsera, Michel. *Zen Macrobiotic Cooking*. Albyn Press, London, 1969.

Alexander, Stephanie. *The Cook's Companion*. Viking, Melbourne, 1996; (2nd edn) Lantern, Melbourne, 2004.

—— *Feasts and Stories*. Allen & Unwin, Sydney, 1988.

Barnes, Julian. *The Pedant in the Kitchen*. Atlantic Books, London, 2003.

Beer, Maggie. *Maggie's Orchard*. Viking, Melbourne, 1997.

Bertolli, Paul. *Cooking by Hand*. Clarkson Potter Publishers, New York, 2003.

Bilson, Gay. *Plenty: Digressions on Food*. Lantern, Melbourne, 2004.

Bilson, Tony. *Tony Bilson's Recipe Book*. William Heinemann, Melbourne, 1987.

Bugialli, Guiliano. *Bugialli on Pasta*. Simon & Schuster, New York, 1998.

Cipriani, Arrigo. *The Harry's Bar Cookbook*. Smith Gryphon, London, 1991.

Cribb, J.W. and A.B. *Wild Food in Australia*. William Collins, Sydney, 1975.

CWA Cookery Book and Household Hints (52 edn). Angus & Robertson, Sydney, 2003.

David, Elizabeth. *English Bread and Yeast Cookery*. Penguin, Harmondsworth, 1997.

Fearnley-Whittingstall, Hugh. *The River Cottage Cookbook*. HarperCollins, London, 2001.

Feniger, Susan and Milliken, Mary Sue. *City Cuisine*. Morrow, New York, 1989.

Field, Carol. *The Italian Baker*. Harper & Row, New York, 1985.

Fisher, M.F.K. *Consider the Oyster*. North Point Press, San Francisco, 1941.

—— *With Bold Knife and Fork*. Putman Publishing Group, New York, 1968.

Herbert, David. *The Perfect Cookbook*. Penguin, Melbourne, 2003.

Hopkinson, Simon. *Roast Chicken and Other Stories*. Ebury Press, London, 1994.

Kurlansky, Mark. *Choice Cuts*. Jonathon Cape, London, 2002.

Levy Beranbaum, Rose. *Pie and Pastry Bible*. Scribner, New York, 1998.

Patten, Marguerite. *Jams, Chutneys, Preserves, Vinegars and Oils*. Bloomsbury, London, 1995.

Petrini, Carlo. *Slow Food: collected writings on taste, tradition and the honest pleasures of food*. Grub Street, London, 2003.

Roden, Claudia. *The Book of Jewish Food*. Alfred A. Knopf, New York, 1996.

Rolls, Eric. *A Celebration of Food and Wine, of Flesh, of Fish, of Fowl*. University of Queensland Press, Brisbane, 1997.

Slater, Nigel. *Toast: the story of a boy's hunger*. Fourth Estate, London, 2000.

Studd, Will. *Chalk and Cheese*. Purple Egg, Melbourne, 1999.

True Food Network (www.greenpeace.org.au/truefood). *The True Food Guide*. Greenpeace, Sydney, 2005.

Waters, Alice. *Chez Panisse Fruit*. HarperCollins, New York, 2002.

Waters, Alice with Bertolli, Paul. *Chez Panisse Cooking*. Random House, New York, 1988.

Witty, Helen and Colchie, Elizabeth Schneider. *Better than Store Bought*. Harper & Row, New York, 1979.

Wright, Elizabeth. *Aromatherapy Soap Making*. Earth Garden Magazine, Good Life Book Club, nd.

Index